MURDERS
THAT SHOCKED
THE WORLD

CASES FROM THE:
1970s

MICHAEL COWTON

BANOVALLUM
BOOKS

Published in Great Britain in 2020
by Banovallum Books
an imprint of Mortons Books Ltd.
Media Centre
Morton Way
Horncastle LN9 6JR
www.mortonsbooks.co.uk

ISBN 978 1 911658 28 3

Typeset by Kelvin Clements

Printed and bound in Great Britain by CPI

*This book is dedicated to the memory of all
those who were denied the opportunity
to count all the sunsets in their lives.*

CONTENTS

MURDERS THAT SHOCKED THE WORLD

CASES FROM THE 1970S

INTRODUCTION

'SOCIETY WANTS to believe it can identify evil people, or bad or harmful people, but it's not practical. There are no stereotypes' Words that may have been uttered by a psychologist, perhaps? Makes sense, doesn't it? But no. They came out of the mouth of Ted Bundy, one of the most notorious serial killers of all time. Here's another of his lines: 'I don't feel guilty for anything. I feel sorry for people who feel guilt.' And most chillingly: 'I'm as cold a motherfucker as you've ever put your fucking eyes on. I don't give a shit about those people.' These are words that summarise the traits of a psychopath: a callous, exploitative individual with blunted emotions, impulsive inclinations and an inability to feel guilt or remorse. Words that sum up the serial killers detailed in this book. Individuals who lacked empathy and compassion; individuals who lacked a deep attachment to others; individuals who had an inflated sense of self-worth and exuded superficial charm. Traits that comprise affective features, interpersonal features, impulsive and antisocial behaviours, whether they be through dishonesty, manipulation or reckless risk taking. In essence, the murderers depicted in the following pages did not care about people, or society, or the good of mankind.

While there are many defining characteristics of the 1970s, serial killers were to play a large part in the narrative. The decade was to become a breeding ground for sadistic murderers. People who haunted the public's imagination with their monikers—Killer Clown, Son of Sam, Hillside Strangler, Yorkshire Ripper—who committed appalling crimes, which often included rape, torture and strangulation. People like Ted Bundy, a handsome, articulate former law student who did not otherwise conform to the typical psychopath stereotype. Others would forge their way into popular myth, such as Jim Jones, the founder of the People's Temple religious movement, who led his followers towards the largest mass murder-suicide in history. They were forced to drink cyanide-laced Kool-Aid, their 'leader' happily contaminating their minds with his own fanaticism and oblique sense of ideology.

While it is not known what drives a person to become a serial killer, it is thought that genetic influence plays a role, alongside environmental and interpersonal factors. Early life experiences such as poor, inconsistent parenting and physical abuse or neglect have also been shown to increase the risk of someone becoming a psychopath. And while it is true that most serial killers are psychopaths, driven by their manipulative, aggressive and impulsive behaviour and blunted emotions, the vast majority of psychopaths are not serial killers. Despite their lack of emotion, the latter can be productive members of society. It is also important to note that many horrendous crimes were committed not by psychopaths but psychotics, who have different kinds of mental disorders and differ in terms of whether they are in touch with reality. Psychosis is a complete loss of one's sense of reality, while psychopathy is a personality disorder, much like narcissistic personality disorder. The killers in this book were, by and large, calculating and manipulative individuals who would show neither guilt nor remorse for their crimes.

As a decade, the 1970s was without question newsworthy, particularly for its negative press. Any sense of optimism was overshadowed by events such as Richard Nixon's ordering of an invasion of Cambodia, widening the war in Vietnam, before he was to become embroiled in Watergate. Pop lovers went into mourning at the announcement of The Beatles' split, and Janis Joplin, Jimi Hendrix and Elvis Presley died. The public endured power cuts and strikes. Patty Hearst, daughter of the American publishing magnate William Randolph Hurst, was kidnapped by the left-wing terrorist group, the Symbionese Liberation Army. What a change from the previous decade, which had witnessed a revolutionary new movement in the underground alternative youth culture, often referred to as the hippy phenomenon, which saw thousands of disaffected teenagers morphing into bohemians, ready to cast off conservative values and instead embrace the opportunity to experiment with sex and drugs. Hairy, hippy, happy gatherings swayed to the sounds of psychedelic music. Come 1969, the wheels had fallen off when the notorious Manson Family murders both shocked and captivated the public. We were then catapulted into what was to become a decade of fear: John Wayne Gacy plagued Chicago; David Berkowitz terrorised New York; Kenneth Bianchi and his cousin Angelo Buono spread fear across Los Angeles as one and the same Hillside Strangler; Peter Sutcliffe brought fear across central Britain; and the deeds of Jim Jones would bookmark a decade contaminated by murder and mass suicide.

With a lack of large-scale computerised databases and DNA not available until the mid-1980s, authorities found themselves fighting a primitive war and were more often than not treading blancmange as they fought the rise in serial killers, a term credited to the late Robert Ressler, an investigator with the Behavioural Science Unit of the FBI who pioneered the practice of criminal profiling. In his 1992 memoir, *Whoever Fights Monsters*, Ressler writes that in the early 1970s, while attending a week-long conference at a British police academy, he heard a fellow participant refer to 'crimes in series', meaning 'a series of rapes, burglaries, arsons or murders'. So impressed was Ressler by the phrase that he began to use the term 'serial killer' in his own lectures to describe 'the killing of those who do one murder, then another and another in a fairly repetitive way'. Along with his colleague John Douglas, Ressler was to serve as a model for the character Jack Crawford in Thomas Harris's Hannibal Lecter trilogy, Red Dragon, The Silence of the Lambs and Hannibal.

Without question, infamous monikers, handles and sobriquets sell newspapers. Since the dawn of the tabloid sensationalist headline, criminal nomenclature—the likes of Doctor Death, The Black Panther or Angel of Death—have struck both fear and revulsion in our souls because we know the context in which they are used, even if we do not know the real names behind them. Nicknames are how serial killers gain notoriety. It is worth noting that the names have a particular structure, usually featuring the ordinary juxtaposed with the extraordinary. This fact is noted by Tom Clark of the University of Sheffield. In his paper, 'Jack's Back: Toward a Sociological Understanding of Serial Killer Nicknames', he writes that while symbolically serving to sustain and alleviate both order and disorder, such nicknames also represent a reminder of the ongoing threat to the normative ideals of contemporary society, while also implying that this threat can be overcome.

The 1970s and 1980s are remembered as the serial killer's heyday, when monsters like David Berkowitz, John Wayne Gacy and Ted Bundy roamed the streets. Bundy's own defence attorney said his client was 'the very definition of heartless evil'. Since then, data suggests the number of serial killers has fallen by as much as 85 per cent in three decades. There are several reasons cited for the decline, including longer prison sentences and a reduction in parole, better forensic science, and cultural and technological shifts. As this has supposedly fallen, so too has the rate of murder cases solved. In the United States for example, in 1965 the number of solved murder cases stood at 91 per cent. By 2017 that figure had fallen to 61.6 per cent, one of the lowest rates in the Western world. Look at that another way: murderers get away with murder about 40 per cent of the time, with some experts believing that serial killers are responsible for a significant number of these unsolved crimes. Several killers in this book were known to roam vast areas of their respective countries, making it harder for the authorities to join up the dots. Catching them sometimes was just down to plain, good old-fashioned luck. David Berkowitz was busted over a random parking ticket. And there's a certain level of irony in the fact that Ted Bundy, the man who successfully escaped prison on several occasions that it must have seemed like he would never be convicted and jailed for good, was caught driving a stolen car in Florida during his last escape from custody. The officer who stopped him initially had no idea who he was.

The likes of Ted Bundy, David Berkowitz and Peter Sutcliffe made up just part of a frightening tapestry of new-age violence as the 1970s became a breeding ground for sadistic killers, born out of an era corrupted by drugs and violence which in turn jump-started a trend in exploitative killer films primed to shock. Violence, horror and smut rippled across nations. Out of the swamp arose such classics (I use the word advisedly) as The Texas Chainsaw

Massacre, A Nightmare On Elm Street, and Friday the 13th, films fixated in the public's psyche. Cheap horror, gore and those nerve-tingling moments of expectancy sell. However, most serial killers are often your quiet next-door neighbour, the shy, retiring sort who keeps himself to himself. Your average Joe. They are not vampires or werewolves or revenants, so forget any morbid fascination for the undead. They don't have supernatural powers at their disposal either and that is precisely why they are so terrifying. They are human beings influenced and determined by a singular twisted logic, acted out in a graveyard of shadows, preying on an innocent public.

Michael Cowton

CHAPTER 1

DAVID BERKOWITZ

THE SON OF SAM

'At this time, I had made a pact with the Devil, I had allowed this satanic thing to control me, and I felt these paranormal powers.'—David Berkowitz.

NEW YORK City, mid-1970s. A city undergoing change. An edgy city of graffiti, looting, gonzo journalism, painting and poetry, lurching towards modernity as the anarchic glam rock of the New York Dolls and the hard-core punk of The Ramones fill the airwaves. Stop a woman unexpectedly in the street and you could be taken down by a face full of Mace. But it wasn't so much the aerosol spray that was bringing the city to its knees in the summer of 1976. No. Rather, people were being gunned down as they sat in their cars. Innocents, going about their ordinary lives in a disorderly world; slowly being marginalised and squeezed out to the suburbs as the inhabitants of once arty enclaves such as Manhattan's East Village saw the light when it came to earning a fast buck and as a consequence started to push up rents. Brooklyn was a different place then. The Italians and Irish were there, and the Puerto Ricans were drifting through. It was all about immigrants. It was working-class. If you happened to be uncomfortable with that, it was not a smart place to be. But rents were decent, so it was possible to work and raise a family without the need to go out and grab yourself a college degree.

Richard David Falco entered this world on June 1, 1953. The result of an affair between Elizabeth 'Betty' Broder and Joseph Klineman, his impoverished Jewish mother had already separated from Klineman by the time her son was born. Some sources believe Klineman, who was already married, threatened to abandon his lover if she kept the child and used his name. So, just days after the birth the baby was put up for adoption. Jewish-American hardware store retailers Nathan and Pearl Berkowitz entered Richard's life, switching his first and middle names and giving him their surname. Home was a middle-class household in The Bronx. While the couple doted on their son, the young Berkowitz grew to resent the fact he had been adopted. He became antisocial and showed little capacity for academia, far preferring to swing a bat in a game of baseball. As he grew up, he earned a reputation for being aggressive and a neighbourhood bully. Concerned at their son's wayward personality, his adoptive parents resorted to consulting a psychotherapist. The relationship between child and adopted mother was, however, rock solid. So close, in fact, that the young Berkowitz became jealous of the attention she foisted on a pet parakeet, so he reportedly poisoned the innocent bird. The first big negative came when Pearl, the woman who had raised him since he was three years old, died in 1967 from a re-occurrence of breast cancer. Aged just 14, Berkowitz felt utterly lost and abandoned, and sank into a deep depression. This is when the mind games came into play. As far as he was concerned, her death had been a master plot designed to destroy him.

From 1969 to 1971 Berkowitz attended Christopher Columbus High School, a public secondary school located in the Pelham Parkway section of The Bronx, within walking distance of the Bronx Zoo and the New York Botanical Garden. He was of above average intelligence, but his schoolwork continued to suffer and his lonely outlook on life intensified. He became fixated on rebellious habits and began to dabble in larceny and pyromania, although his misbehaviour never led to trouble with law enforcement or impacted on his school records. He did not fare much better when he was switched to Bronx Community College, a historic campus atop a hill overlooking the Harlem River. Neither did it work out for him at SUNY Sullivan, a public community college in Loch Sheldrake, in New York's Sullivan County, a small, rural town mostly populated by young professionals. He might have expected things to change when his adoptive father remarried in 1971 but there was tension between the new woman in the house and the young Berkowitz. The final straw came when his father and his second wife decided to relocate to Florida. Angry and confused, 18-year-old Berkowitz was left behind to fend for himself. The messed-up dynamic between himself and the adults in his life would go on to have a profound effect on his future.

In 1971, he joined the U.S. Army and served in America and South Korea, where he excelled as a proficient marksman. Honourably discharged from military service in 1974, Berkowitz returned to New York and picked up a job as a letter sorter for the U.S. Postal Service. It was around this time that he tracked down his birth mother, whom Berkowitz originally believed had died in childbirth. During a brief reunion, Betty Falco told him about his illegitimate birth. He discovered that his birth father was dead and had not wanted to play any role in his son's upbringing. A despondent, lonely Berkowitz found his mother was distant, so he stopped the all-too-brief interactions, his sense of personal identity destroyed. According to Elliot Leyton, a forensic anthropologist who would later study the case, Berkowitz was hugely affected by the truth about his birth and went to categorise this discovery as the 'primary crisis' of the killer's life. Berkowitz eventually lost contact with his mother and began working several blue-collar jobs. Co-workers described him as a loner who kept to himself. Then something snapped in his head: he believed he was unwanted not only by his real mother, but by all women. His isolation was complete. Denied friendship, denied a girlfriend, denied sex, denied happiness, denied anything and everything.

Christmas Eve, 1975. Fifteen-year-old Michelle Forman and a friend were walking along a New York City street. According to his accounts, Berkowitz approached them from behind with a hunting knife and stabbed them in the back. Fortunately, they survived, and Forman was treated for knife wounds. The teenagers were unable to identify their attacker. It had started. Soon after the attack Berkowitz moved into an apartment in Yonkers, a city on the Hudson River in Westchester County, New York. An attractive area with parks and gardens, water features and river views. Not that Berkowitz probably took much notice. He was more disturbed by the neighbourhood dogs that kept him awake at night. Their incessant howls were messages from demons ordering him to kill women. Believing that the couple who owned the house were part of the conspiracy against him, he moved to an apartment on Pine Street, only for those same demons to follow. Sam Carr, his neighbour, had a pet Labrador named Harvey. To Berkowitz, the dog was possessed. Having acquired a .44 calibre Charter Arms Bulldog revolver in Texas, he shot the animal.

Shortly after 1am on July 29, 1976, 18-year-old Donna Lauria and 19-year-old student nurse Jody Valenti were sitting in Valenti's two-door blue Oldsmobile Cutlass. It was double parked in front of the Lauria family's six-storey apartment building at 2860 Buhre Avenue in the Westchester

Heights section of The Bronx, only a short distance from where Valenti lived at 1918 Hutchinson River Parkway. The friends had spent a fun night dancing at a disco in New Rochelle. It was what teenagers did then, with New York City having turned into disco central, and with no small thanks to John Travolta as Brooklyn dance king Tony Manero in *Saturday Night Fever*, the seminal film of the time. They had run into Lauria's parents and pleasantries were exchanged. After the adults retired inside, the girls chatted about plans for the summer. It was then that a stranger in a striped shirt walked to within about 8ft of the car. As Lauria turned to Valenti to ask if she knew who the person was, four shots shattered the vehicle's closed window. Lauria, who was partway through training as a New York City medic, was killed instantly from a bullet in the back. Valenti took a bullet in the left thigh and survived. When questioned by police, she stated that she did not recognise the attacker but was able to give them a description—male, about 30 years old, white, with curly hair. These details fitted with a statement by Lauria's father, who told how he had seen a man of the same description sitting in a yellow car. Other individuals in the neighbourhood testified that they had seen a yellow car driving around the area on the night of the shooting. Police determined that the gun used was a .44 calibre Charter Arms Bulldog revolver.

The next day, when Berkowitz happened to pick up a newspaper, he realised he had made his first killing. 'I was literally singing to myself on my way home, after the killing.

The tension, the desire to kill a woman, had built up in such explosive proportions that when I finally pulled the trigger, all the pressures, all the tensions, all the hatred, had just vanished, dissipated, but only for a short time,' he was to state later.

As far as the police was concerned, it appeared to have been a random shooting and all part of the violence permeating the darker side of a declining city. A fellow prisoner asked Berkowitz years later how he happened to target the girls. 'I just pulled by them,' he replied. 'I parked around the corner and came out and did it.' It was 40 years before Jodi Valenti broke her silence about that night, telling Jenny Oppenheimer in an interview for the New York Post on July 17, 2016: 'It took probably six years of my life to be able to get in a car at night. It took a long time to be able to deal with the sounds of popping fireworks and stuff like that... but I faced my fears.' And face them she did, learning how to shoot a gun at a time unprecedented in America, when gun violence was beginning to run rampant.

During the 1970s, a Chinese community established a foothold in the neighbourhood of Flushing, in the borough of Queens, whose demographic constituency had been predominantly non-Hispanic white, interspersed with a small Japanese community. A wave of immigrants from Taiwan was the first to arrive and develop Flushing's Chinatown, which soon became known as Little Taipei or Little Taiwan. A large South Korean population also called Flushing home, and it was here that, on October 23, 1976, Berkowitz struck again. Carl Denaro, a 20-year-old who wore his hair long, was sitting in his red VW in Queens with his girlfriend, 18-year-old Rosemary Keenan, when shots rang out and the car window shattered. Keenan promptly started the car and drove off. It was not until they managed to get help that the couple realised they'd been shot at, despite Denaro having a bullet wound in his head. Both survived the attack and neither saw their assailant. Police later found that the bullets were .44 calibre but could not determine what gun they came from. Investigators also initially failed to make a connection between this shooting and the previous one, for the simple fact that they had occurred in two separate boroughs.

There were more incidents. Lots more. Berkowitz's killing spree was to continue for a year. New York City went into lockdown. Shortly after midnight on November 27, 1976, 16-year-old Donna DeMasi and 18-year-old Jody Lomino were talking on the stoop of Lomino's home on 262nd Street in Floral Park, having watched a late movie. Berkowitz, wearing military fatigues, had spotted them. He asked them for directions, then drew a gun and opened fire. They survived, although Lomino was left paralysed for life. Police again determined that the bullets were from an unknown .44 calibre gun and were able to make composite sketches based on testimonies from the girls and neighbourhood witnesses.

January 30, 1977. Outside the Forest Hills Inn in Queens. Newly engaged Christine Freund, aged 26, and her fiancé, 30-year-old John Diel, were shot as they sat chatting in his Pontiac Firebird. Freund was killed and Diel survived. Another desperate tragedy, and the police soon pounced on their first real clue. They ascertained that the bullet that had ended Freund's life had been fired from a .44-caliber Charter Arms Bulldog revolver, and the shooter seemed to target young women with long, dark hair. The Press seized on the fact, dubbing the shooter 'The .44-Calibre Killer'. When the composite sketches from the various attacks were released, NYPD officials noted they were likely searching for multiple shooters. A reasonable assumption based on the evidence to date, but how wrong they were.

Weeks later, on March 8, 1977, 21-year-old Columbia University student Virginia Voskerichian was killed while walking home from class. She lived one block away from fellow victim Christine Freund. Voskerichian was shot several times, and eventually died of a gunshot wound to the head. In the minutes following the shooting, a neighbour who heard the gunfire went outside and saw what he described as a short, husky, teenage boy sprinting from the crime scene. Other neighbours also reported seeing the teenager and a man matching Berkowitz's description in the area. Early media coverage implied that the teenager was the perpetrator. Eventually, however, police officials determined the teenager was a witness and not a suspect. On April 17, 1977, Alexander Esau and Valentina Suriani were in The Bronx, several blocks away from the scene of the Valenti-Lauria shooting. The couple were each shot twice while sitting in a car, and both died before they could talk to police. Investigators determined that they were killed by the same suspect, with the same .44 calibre firearm. At the scene, police discovered a handwritten letter addressed to the captain of the NYPD from the killer. He referred to himself as the 'Son of Sam', and expressed a desire to continue his shooting spree. The badly misspelt letter stated: 'I am deeply hurt by your calling me a wemon hater. I am not. But I am a monster. I am the "Son of Sam". I'm a little "brat".' It went on: 'When father Sam gets drunk, he gets mean. He beats his family. Sometimes he ties me up to the back of the house. Other times he locks me in the garage. Sam loves to drink blood. "Go out and kill," commands father Sam. Behind our house some rest. Mostly young—raped and slaughtered—their blood drained—just bones now. Papa Sam keeps me locked in the attic, too. I can't get out, but I look out the attic window and watch the world go by. I feel like an outsider. I am on a different wavelength then everybody.' This taunting letter could quite easily be viewed as delusional nonsense, but any number of incidents in his life may have pushed Berkowitz over the edge. It is not known, either, whether he was referring to 'Sam' as his adopted father, with whom he had a strained relationship. When questioned about the letter after he had been arrested, Berkowitz said that 'Sam' was his next-door neighbour's dog.

Heading up *Operation Omega,* the special task force formed to investigate the killings, was *New York* City police detective Timothy J. Dowd. Dozens of detectives, all seeking the killer before he struck again, were spurred on by the taunting letters to both the department and New York Daily News columnist Jimmy Breslin—those same letters that gave birth to the nickname 'Son of Sam'. Police set about tracking down and questioning every legal owner of a .44 calibre Bulldog revolver in New York City, in addition to forensically testing the guns. Despite their exhaustive trawling, they were unable to determine which was the murder weapon. Traps were also set up, where undercover police officers posed as couples in parked cars in the hope that the suspect would reveal himself. Investigators were also slowly building a psychological profile for the suspect, drawn from information from the first letter and the connections between the previous shootings. Their suspect was described as neurotic, potentially suffering from paranoid schizophrenia, and someone who believed he was possessed by demons.

On May 30, 1977, columnist Jimmy Breslin received a second 'Son of Sam' letter. It was postmarked that same day from Englewood, New Jersey. The envelope had the words 'Blood and Family—Darkness and Death—Absolute Depravity—.44' written on the reverse side. The Son of Sam stated in the letter that he was a reader of Breslin's column and referenced several of the past victims. It asked Breslin how he planned to commemorate the shooting of Donna DeMasi and Jody Lomino: 'What will you have for July 29?' The writer continued to mock the New York City Police Department over its inability to solve the case. Up until now, Berkowitz had been content to sit back and goad the police, and the bizarre letters continued. Chillingly, another message opened with the greeting: 'Hello from the gutters of NYC, which are filled with dog manure, vomit, stale wine, urine and blood… Sam's a thirsty lad and he won't let me stop killing until he gets his fill of blood.' A further letter read: 'Love to hunt. Prowling the streets looking for fair game—tasty meat. The wemon of Queens are z prettyist of all. I must be the water they drink. I live for the hunt—my life. Blood for papa. Mr Borelli, Sir, I don't want to kill anymore no sir, no more but I must, "honour thy father". I want to make love to the world. I love people. I don't belong on earth. Return me to yahoos. To the people of Queens, I love you. And I want to wish all of you a happy Easter. May God bless you in this life and in the next and for now I say goodbye and goodnight. Police—let me haunt you with these words; I'll be back I'll be back to be interpreted as bang, bang, bang, bang, ugh!! Yours in murder Mr. Monster.' Captain Joseph Borrelli, mentioned here, was the head of the homicide unit for Queens.

'What will you have for July 29?' Could this have been a warning? Investigators thought so, particularly as July 29 was the first anniversary of the first shooting. The one noticeable change with this letter was that it appeared to have been written in a more sophisticated manner than the previous one, leading investigators to consider whether a copycat could have penned the words. Published about a week later, the letter's contents sent much of New York City into a panic. Many women opted to change their hairstyle, due to Berkowitz's propensity for attacking women with long dark hair. Different coloured wigs started to fly out of stores. Reds and oranges and blondes… anything but black.

Just past 3am on June 26, 1977, 17-year-old Judy Placido of The Bronx had left a disco in Bayside, Queens, with her friend Sal Lupo. They were sat in Lupo's car when shots riddled the vehicle. Placido was struck three times in the right temple, right shoulder and the back of the neck. Lupo was hit in the right forearm. Incredibly, both survived. Once again, neither knew their attacker. However, witnesses did report seeing a tall, stocky man with dark hair fleeing the crime scene, as well as a blond man with a moustache driving in the area. Police believed the dark-haired man was their suspect, and the blond man was a witness. By the summer of 1977, the victim toll had reached five dead and six injured. Captain Borrelli then received a four-page letter, peppered with allusions to vampires and monsters, warning that the killer would strike again, which heightened the public unease. From the Hamptons to Queens and all New York City boroughs, people were running scared, not knowing when or from where the next hit would come. The police had set up a dragnet in The Bronx and Queens. Those wigs were still selling well. The disco floors were pretty much deserted. People were too terrified to leave their homes at night.

Bath Beach is a neighbourhood in Brooklyn, located at the south-western edge of the borough on Gravesend Bay. It was so-called for the British spa town of Bath. In the late 1800s, Brooklyn's nabobs and elite used the place as a

Hamptons-like summer resort with their villas, yacht clubs and mansions. After the stock market crash in 1929, things changed. The elite moved further east on Long Island and Jewish and Italian immigrants moved in, to be joined later by Asians and Latinos. Small family shops and chain stores line today's streets. Unless you have a home here, there seems little reason to visit. The beach has gone too—paved over to make the Belt Highway, although you can still walk the waterfront promenade. It was in this neighbourhood that the 'Son of Sam' struck for the final time.

Presumably conscious of the police dragnet, for the first time Berkowitz switched his attention to Brooklyn. On July 31, 1977, two days after the anniversary of the first shooting, he struck again. Stacy Moskowitz and Robert Violante were in Violante's car, parked up near a public park, when a man walked up to the passenger side and began shooting. Moskowitz suffered a gunshot wound to the head and died at hospital. Violante survived, but lost vision in one eye and partial vision in the other. Unlike most of the other female victims, Moskowitz did not have long or dark hair.

Fortuitously, several witnesses provided descriptions of the shooter. One said the man looked like he was wearing a wig, which could well account for the varying descriptions of suspects with blond and dark hair. Several others saw a man matching the killer's description wearing a wig and speeding away from the scene in a yellow car without headlights. Police decided to investigate the owners of any yellow cars matching the description. Although Berkowitz's car was one of those, investigators initially pegged him as a witness rather than a suspect.

The breakthrough came for the task force when a dog walker remembered seeing an officer, ticketing cars on the night of the shooting. Detective James Justus followed up on this, and one of the tickets had been issued to a David Berkowitz of Yonkers for a Ford Galaxie. The vehicle had been parked too close to a fire hydrant. On August 10 detectives drove to the Yonkers apartment, where they saw the Ford. Inside the car they found a rifle and a duffel bag filled with ammunition, maps of the crime scenes and an unsent 'Son of Sam' letter addressed to Sergeant Dowd of the Omega task force. They also found a note, which read:

Because Craig is Craig
So must the streets
Be filled with Craig (death)
And huge drops of lead
Poured down upon his head
Until she is dead.
Yet, the cats still come out
At night to mate
And the sparrows still
Sing in the morning.

The police waited for Berkowitz to leave his apartment, giving them enough time to obtain a warrant because they had searched his car without one. The warrant never arrived, but that didn't deter police from surrounding Berkowitz when he left his home. Detective John Falotico already had a stellar career. As an 18-year-long member of former Manhattan District Attorney Frank Hogan's elite detective squad, he had helped to put away such organised crime figures as Joe Gallo, Joe Bonnano and Carmine Persico. On the night of Berkowitz's arrest, Falotico asked him: 'Now that I've got you, who have I got?' 'You know," Berkowitz replied, in what the detective remembered was a soft, almost sweet voice. 'No, I don't.' Falotico insisted. 'You tell me.' 'I'm Sam.'

In the apartment, officers found satanic graffiti drawn on the walls and diaries detailing Berkowitz's alleged 1,400 arson attacks in the New York area. Upon questioning, he quickly confessed to the shootings and stated he would plead guilty. When asked what his motivation for the killing spree was, he told police that his former neighbour, Sam Carr, had a dog that was possessed by a demon, which told Berkowitz to kill. It transpired that Sam Carr was the same Sam that inspired his 'Son of Sam' nickname. When interviewed by FBI veteran Robert Ressler in February 1979, Berkowitz admitted inventing the 'Son of Sam' stories so that if he was caught, he could convince the court that he was insane. 'It was all a hoax, a silly hoax' he told Dr David Abrahamsen, a court-appointed psychiatrist, and said he lashed out in anger against a world he felt had rejected him—particularly women. Four psychiatrists assessed Berkowitz, and three found him mentally unfit to stand trial. The fourth opined that he was sane. The resulting case went on to become a prominent example of the controversy surrounding the insanity defence. In that same month of February, Berkowitz held a press conference and stated that his claims about demonic possession had all been a hoax.

Berkowitz appeared before Justice Joseph R. Corso of the State Supreme Court on May 22. Following a wild-eyed tirade against his victims and their families, the accused was dragged from the courtroom and Justice Corso ordered a new psychiatric examination to determine Berkowitz's fitness to be sentenced. Doctors Richard Wridenbacher and Daniel Schwartz of the Kings County Medical Centre, the two forensic psychiatrists concerned, concluded that he was indeed fit for sentencing. Reporting in The New York Times on June 13, 1978, Max H. Seigel stated that 25-year-old Berkowitz appeared calm and subdued as he entered the same Brooklyn courtroom he threw into turmoil three weeks before. The same could hardly be said for one of the spectators. Daniel Carrique, a friend of victim Stacy Moskowitz's family, had interrupted proceedings at the previous hearing and erupted again. He leaped from his sixth-row seat to clamber over benches and spectators to get to Berkowitz, shouting: 'You're going to burn in hell. You're going to burn, Berkowitz. I'll get you.' He was led from the courtroom by officers and later charged with assault and obstructing justice.

Justice Corso opened the procedure under which three Supreme Court justices from three different counties in the city where the murders were committed would each sentence the defendant. District Attorney Eugene Gold recommended the maximum sentence. Leon Stern, Berkowitz's lawyer, moved to set aside both his client's guilty plea and the sentencing on the grounds that the defendant 'by reason of his mental defects' was incapable of taking part in the procedure. Justice Corso denied both motions, having referred to reports from psychiatrists. When Berkowitz said he had no statement, Justice Corso sentenced him to 25 years to life for the murder of Miss Moskowitz and up to 25 years for the attempted murder of Robert Violante, the sentences to run consecutively. Justice Nicholas Tsoucalas of Queens then sentenced Berkowitz to up to 25 years in prison for wounding Carl Denaro, in Flushing, Queens, and to a consecutive sentence of up to 25 years for the assault on Mr. Denaro's companion, Rosemary Keenan. For the attempted murder of Judy Placido and Salvatore Lupo, in Bayside, Queens, Justice Tsoucalas imposed two 25-year terms, plus 15 years for assault, all to run consecutively. Finally, the justice sentenced Berkowitz to 25 years to life for the murder of Christine Freund, 25 years for the attempted murder of John Diel and 25 years to life for the murder of Virginia Voskerichian. All sentences were to run consecutively. 'As is obvious by the sentences of this court,' said Justice Tsoucalas, 'it is the object of this court that the defendant be incarcerated for the rest of his natural life.'

Justice William Kapelman of The Bronx, who was present to sentence Berkowitz for three murders and one attempted murder in that borough, said that while the consecutive sentences imposed by the other justices had popular appeal and were permissible, the fact was that they would be 'merged' for the purpose of 'determining how long a prisoner remained in custody before being eligible for parole'. As a result, Berkowitz would be eligible after 25 years—no matter for how long he was sentenced. He then imposed maximum sentences of 25 years to life for the murder of Valentina Suriani and Alexander Esau in the Baychester section of The Bronx, and for the murder of Donna Laurie. For the attempted murder of Jody Valenti, he imposed a sentence of 25 years, all to run concurrently, with the sentences imposed by other justices. After sentencing, Justice Corso disclosed that he would have sent Berkowitz to the electric chair if that option had been available. 'I think that if we had capital punishment,' he said, 'it would have been a deterrent to the obviously absolutely senseless killings that come into my courtroom.' Having pleaded guilty to six murders, Berkowitz was sentenced to a total of 365 years in prison without possibility of parole, to be served in Upstate New York's supermax prison, the Attica Correctional Facility. He instructed his lawyers not to appeal.

On July 10, 1979, Berkowitz was giving out water to other prisoners in his section when inmate William E. Hauser attacked him with a razor blade and slashed his throat. Berkowitz was too afraid to cooperate with the resultant investigation, despite that it almost cost him his life. Hauser's name was not released to the public until 2015, when it was revealed by Attica superintendent James Conway.

Having refused to attend any of his parole hearings since he became eligible for possible release in 2002, in May 2016 Berkowitz changed his mind. Aged 63 at the time, he told the parole board: 'I was constantly putting myself out there to help other individuals, with kindness and compassion. I mean, I feel that's my life's calling, all these years. My evaluations, and so forth, should show that to be true. I've done a lot of good and positive things, and I thank God for that.'

Today, Berkowitz is an evangelical born-again Christian and described as a model prisoner. An official website run by his supporters claims this 'former Son of Sam' is now 'the Son of Hope', as seen in his book, Son of Hope: The Prison Journals of David Berkowitz, published in 2006. 'The people and the news media used to call me The Son of Sam, but God has given me a new name, The Son of Hope, because now my life is about hope,' he stated. In his book and on the website, Berkowitz provides an apology to his victims and their families. In prison, he continues to write journal essays on faith and repentance, as well as contribute to school-based projects for students in psychology, criminology and sociology who want to learn more about the criminal mind and the criminal justice system. Berkowitz has been offered substantial sums of money to share his story. However, nearly all states—including New York—have since passed legislation, sometimes known as 'Son of Sam laws', that prohibits criminals from financially profiting from their story through books, films or other enterprises related to their crimes, by selling memoirs or being paid when their stories are adapted. Although there are numerous media renditions of the 'Son of Sam' case, Berkowitz does not financially profit from any works by him or anyone else.

In a CBS News special entitled Son of Sam: The Killer Speaks, broadcast on Friday, August 11, 2017, Berkowitz spoke of what led him to kill, his life before he turned into a murderer and life in prison. He told correspondent Maurice DuBois that people would never understand where he came from, no matter how much he tried to explain it: 'They wouldn't understand what it was like to walk in darkness.' While living alone in Yonkers, he felt isolated, although he didn't see it at the time: 'I was just very lost and confused. There was a battle going on inside me.' The shootings, he said, were 'a break from reality, thought I was doing something to appease the devil. I'm sorry for it.'

There has been some speculation about the actual single shooter theory, with officials involved in the case sowing seeds of doubt. John Santucci, Queens District Attorney at the time Berkowitz was operating, and police investigator Mike Novotny have both since expressed their convictions that he had accomplices. The fact that there were discrepancies in witness and victim statements have raised suspicions that Berkowitz did not operate alone. NYPD officer Richard Johnson noted: 'Why are there three (suspect) cars, five different (suspect) descriptions, different heights, different shapes, different sizes of the perpetrator? Somebody else was there.' Journalist Maury Terry, writing for the Gannett newspapers in 1979, also challenged the official explanation of a lone gunman. Her articles were later be compiled in book form as The Ultimate Evil, which first went to print in 1987. No doubt spurred on by circulating reports of accomplices and satanic cult activity, the Berkowitz case was re-opened in 1996 by Yonkers police, although ultimately no new charges were filed, and the case was suspended. However, despite a lack of findings by investigating officers, the case remains open and still in people's minds, no doubt due to the number of works published since the trial. Less than a year after Berkowitz's arrest, Jimmy Breslin collaborated with writer Dick Schaap on a novelised account of the murders, entitled .44, which was renamed Son of Sam outside North America. Burn Baby Burn by Meg Medina, published in 2016, is set in New York during the campaign of terror and depicts how the fear of being one of Berkowitz's victims affected the daily lives of New Yorkers. Spike Lee wrote the drama Summer of Sam, which was released in 1999, and other film portrayals include the Ulli Lommel DVD release Son of Sam in 2008, the CBS television film Out of the Darkness in 1985 and the mini series of 2007 titled The Bronx is Burnin'.

Berkowitz is currently incarcerated at the maximum security Shawangunk Correctional Facility in Wallkill, New York, after having been transferred from Sullivan Correctional Facility in Fallsburg, New York, where he spent several years. On December 12, 2017, the state Department of Correctional Services revealed he had been transferred to Albany Medical Centre, an outside hospital. Although officials would not offer specific medical details, the *New York Post* and the *Times-Union* of Albany reported that Berkowitz was to undergo emergency heart surgery. 'Inmate Berkowitz has been transferred to an outside hospital and remains in the custody of the Shawangunk Correctional Facility,' read a statement from the New York Department of Corrections and Community Supervision. 'DOCCS cannot comment on an inmate's specific medical condition' declared the Times-Union. In February 2018, the New York Post reported that Berkowitz had suffered a heart attack prior to his first operation in the December. He was re-admitted later that same month for a procedure to address clotting and improve circulation in his legs. His lawyer, Mark Heller, told Carl Campanile of the New York Post that Berkowitz had responded well to treatment after complications had set in. 'David was optimistic. He said God was watching over him. He's a very spiritual person,' said Heller.

Back in April 2, 2002, Berkowitz posted an open letter online to his victims, apologising for the 'pain, grief and suffering that I have put you through', stating that he regretted how his actions had torn their lives apart, and hoped and prayed that they would heal as much as possible and get on with their lives. If only life was that simple.

CHAPTER 2

THEODORE ROBERT COWELL (TED BUNDY)

THE LADY KILLER

'We serial killers are your sons, we are your husbands,
we are everywhere. And there will be more of
your children dead tomorrow.'— Ted Bundy.

'BURN, BUNDY, BURN' exclaimed the signs held aloft by howling protestors. We will never know if Ted Bundy heard the cries, although he would have been well aware of the commotion occurring outside the gates of Florida State Prison. January 24, 1989. Another hot day, normal for the time of year in the Sunshine State, with average temperatures peaking at 82°F. The average overnight temperature had been unusually warmer, but it is doubtful whether the locals were conscious or even bothered by it. They—and one might think the whole world—was zeroed in on a national event, eager to see justice served on a man who had brutally murdered at least 30 people. One of his victims was Kimberly Leach. Bundy had kidnapped the 12-year-old from her school in Lake City, killed her and dumped her body in Suwannee State Park.

The night before Bundy's execution, he twice called his mother, who refused to believe the charges against her son until he confessed. Those phone calls were perhaps his last hurrah, during which time he was handed his last meal on earth—nothing lavish, a concoction of steak, eggs, hash browns and toast. He let it go cold, uneaten. There probably seemed little point in drawing his final breath on a full stomach. The US Supreme Court had reinstated the death penalty in 1976. As of May 31, 2019, Bundy was one of 1,499 people executed those past 43 years. While the number of death row inmates changes daily with new convictions, appellate decisions overturning conviction or sentence alone, commutations, or deaths (through execution or otherwise), as of June 20, 2019, there were 2,635 people on death row. Florida is one of eight states that carry out executions, the others being Alabama, Arizona, Arkansas, California, Colorado, Georgia and Idaho. Like many death row inmates across the U.S., Bundy spent years in prison before execution by electric chair. In 2010, a death row inmate waited about 15 years between sentencing and execution, and almost a quarter died of natural causes while awaiting their ultimate punishment. Bundy had been counting the days down for nine years before he was put to death by the state.

Theodore Robert Cowell was born on November 24, 1946 at the Elizabeth Lund Home for Unwed Mothers in Burlington to 22-year-old Eleanor 'Louise' Cowell. She originally planned to place her son up for adoption but two months after the birth, unmarried Louise returned to her parents in Philadelphia to raise her first-born. The father's identity has never been determined with any degree of certainty. Ann Rule, a co-worker of Bundy and the author of the book The Stranger Beside Me, The True Crime Story of Ted Bundy, notes it may have been Lloyd Marshall, an Air Force veteran and a Penn State graduate. Other sources name his biological father as Jack Worthington, while other rumours had it that his father was also his grandfather. It is doubtful that the truth will ever be known, and Bundy's birth certificate listed his father as unknown. Louise's parents were deeply religious and the illegitimate birth of a grandchild no doubt brought humiliation upon the household. In a convoluted lie, Bundy was said to be the adopted son of his grandparents and was told that his mother was his sister. However, in her book, Rule said Bundy told her he'd seen through the lie. 'Maybe I just figured out that there couldn't be 20 years' difference in age between a brother and a sister, and Louise always took care of me. I just grew up knowing that she was really my mother.'

Outwardly, life for the Cowells was normal but behind closed doors was a different story. Bundy's grandmother suffered from depression and agoraphobia, and his grandfather was known to have a temper. It is not known whether the young Theodore was the recipient of physical or psychological abuse at the hands of his grandfather, as he later insisted that the two enjoyed a good relationship. When Bundy was three years old, his mother took him to live in Tacoma, Washington, giving him the surname of Nelson to hide that he was illegitimate. Here she met and married Army hospital cook John Culpepper Bundy, known as Johnnie, in 1951. A young and impressionable Theodore grew to resent his stepfather, believing him to be too uneducated and working-class for his mother. Even so, Johnnie was happy to adopt the child and give him his name. Louise proved to be the ever-attentive mother but there was continuing tension between stepfather and child, Theodore perhaps resenting that the family income saw him go without the expensive clothes and other accoutrements he so yearned for, and no doubt exacerbated by the fact that there were to be two brothers and a sister to accommodate everyday needs. Bundy's illegitimacy plagued him throughout his teenage years, never having truly believed that Louise was his sister. There are differing versions about how he learned the truth. A psychologist who interviewed Bundy was told he had found his birth certificate. In another account, documented in the book Phantom Prince, a girlfriend of Bundy's when he was a teenager said he was teased by a cousin about his illegitimacy, using his birth certificate to prove he was right.

Woodrow Wilson High School, a four-year public secondary school and one of five traditional high schools in the Tacoma Public School System, was located at the intersection of Orchard Street and 11th Street. It was here that Bundy graduated in 1965, with predictions of a bright future. He was then awarded a scholarship at the University of Puget Sound, Tacoma, and began taking courses in psychology and oriental studies. Set in a stunning 97 acres, the independent, residential and predominantly undergraduate liberal arts college offered graduate programmes in education and health sciences. By this time, his high school friends had dispersed, and Bundy spent much time alone. After two semesters he decided to transfer to Seattle's University of Washington for his sophomore year, enrolling in an intensive Chinese language programme. According to Rule's book, 'he felt that China was the country that we would one day have to reckon with, and that a fluency in the language would be imperative.' Alongside studying, he worked as a grocery bagger and shelf stocker at a Seattle Safeway store on Queen Anne Hill. But he never held a job for longer than a few months at a time. Though he was not caught stealing at work, employers regarded him with suspicion. During this time, he embarked on his first serious relationship. Diane Edwards (who is often referred to by her alias, Stephanie Brooks) was a wealthy brunette from California. She had class, influence and money—everything the young Ted dreamed of. He drove round in a prized possession, a 1958 Volkswagen Bug, which he bought for $400 and later traded in for a newer, lighter brown 1968 model. His relationship with Edwards was doomed from the outset; he was soon dumped, apparently for a lack of motivation and immaturity. Devastated, Bundy immersed himself in university classes and Republican Party politics. Experts have since believed that the break-up went a long way to explaining why Bundy later chose to rape, beat and murder victims who resembled his ex—a chilling thought. Bundy lost interest in his Chinese studies and instead switched to classes in urban planning and sociology, eventually dropping out altogether. While his first girlfriend went on to graduate with a degree, Bundy took a series of low-paid jobs and was then appointed to the Seattle Crime Prevention Advisory Committee, and later became an assistant to Ross Davis, the chair of the Washington State Republican Party. His experience of studying psychology saw him later work as a night-shift volunteer at Seattle's Suicide Hot Line, a crisis centre serving the greater Seattle metropolitan and suburban areas. Here he met and worked alongside former Seattle policewoman and then fledgling crime writer Ann Rule.

For Bundy, life was all about keeping up appearances. A handsome young man with striking blue eyes, he had a passion for dressing impeccably. But appearances were deceptive. Due to a lack of finances, he began stealing from stores and homes. Having attended theatrical arts classes at university, he had a good grasp of acting and make-up, and was able to change his appearance at will by sporting a false moustache. To feed his habit of deception, while working for a medical supply company he resorted to taking a variety of props, including plaster casting material, splints, slings and crutches. He'd had a habit of peeping into women's bedrooms since childhood, and he also developed an appetite for violent pornography. In 1969, he dated Elizabeth Kloepfer, a divorced secretary with a daughter who fell deeply in love with him, and the relationship only ended when Bundy was jailed for kidnapping in 1976. Restless and with no real sense of direction, in 1969 he travelled around the country, reportedly visiting his hometown of Vermont to learn about his birth parents. Having then taken a semester of classes at Temple University in Philadelphia, he returned to Tacoma to re-enrol at the University of Washington, where he earned a Bachelor of Arts degree in psychology in 1972. There could well be perceived to be a certain element of irony in that. Bundy then briefly attended the new University of Puget Sound Law School for night classes three times a week, before transferring to the University of Utah's law school in Salt Lake City in September 1973, no doubt helped by his political connections. According to the publication Business Insider, the then Washington governor Daniel Evans, whom Bundy worked for, put in a good word for him. It did not help, because only a year later the graduate student dropped out, despite clearly having the acumen for a successful career in politics. According to a Psychology Today report, Bundy aspired to become the next governor of Washington. Instead, he turned his eye to other things: murder. During a business trip to California in the summer of 1973, Bundy came back into the life of his former girlfriend Diane Edwards, known by now as Stephanie Brooks, with a new look and attitude; a serious, dedicated professional accepted into law school. Bundy continued to date Kloepfer too, and neither woman was aware the other existed. Bundy courted Brooks throughout the rest of the year, and she accepted his marriage proposal. Shortly after New Year 1974, he unceremoniously dumped her and refused to return her phone calls. A few weeks after the break-up, Bundy began a murderous rampage in Washington State.

Lynda Ann Healy had grown up in a comfortable suburb outside Seattle with her parents and two siblings, according to the book The Only Living Witness: The True Story of Serial Killer Ted Bundy. In February 1974, the popular 21-year-old University of Washington student and talented musician had entered her senior year and shared a house close to campus with four other women. While her roommates slept soundly, Lynda would rise early and head for the local radio station, where five days a week she read Northwest Ski Reports. One morning she failed to turn up—a fact that did not go unnoticed by Kathleen McChesney, a detective with the King County Police and regular listener of the bulletin. Her disappearance was first noted by roommate Barbara Little, who heard her friend's alarm sounding. When she entered the room, Healy was nowhere to be found. The radio station called the house asking of her whereabouts, and then her roommates noticed other disturbing signs. The back door, which was always kept locked, was open. Nor had anyone seen her on campus the previous afternoon or evening. The Seattle Police Department was notified and when Lieutenant Pat Murphy showed up, he noted that Healy's room was neat, with no sign of foul play... except for some blood on the pillow and head area of the sheets. Then her bloodstained nightgown was discovered in the closet, and her backpack and a pink satin pillowcase were missing. An investigation was launched but having interviewed 65 people, investigators were none the wiser.

In October 1974 three young women unaccountably disappeared from small towns outside Salt Lake City. On November 7, 18-year-old Carol DaRonch had a lucky escape when she was attacked in a shopping mall in Salt Lake City. Bundy approached her and said someone was trying to break into her car. DaRonch assumed he was a police officer, and Bundy later showed her a badge. He asked her to accompany him to the car. She looked inside and confirmed nothing was missing, and Bundy requested that she went to the police station to make a complaint. He drove her in his Volkswagen, pulling over on the way and forcibly placing handcuffs on her wrist. She screamed and fought her way out of the vehicle before escaping.

Connecting the Cedar River Watershed to the Tiger Mountain State Forest, the 1,924-acre Taylor Mountain Forest treats visitors to views of Mount Rainier, forested wetlands and wildflower meadows. Trails and forest service roads cut through the trees and attract horse riders, hikers and mountain bike riders. It was in this area of ecological significance that missing student Lynda Healy's body was discovered in 1975, along with other girls.

In total, nine young women aged between 18 and 22 had vanished from college campuses and recreation areas in Washington and Oregon in early 1974. Only seven bodies were ever recovered, having been left to decompose in wooded areas around Seattle. They had all been assaulted and either bludgeoned or strangled to death. Still with few leads to follow, investigators were drawn to one that pointed to a handsome, polite and friendly man who drove a Volkswagen and introduced himself as Ted. He was noted to wear a cast on his leg and use crutches to hobble around or wear his arm in a cast, supported by a sling. The Pacific Northwest soon went into panic mode—a serial killer was on the loose. The 'Ted Hotline' was burning as hundreds of people called to accuse 'Teds' they knew who owned a Volkswagen and had some vague similarity to the composite pictures running in the media. Husbands, boyfriends, strangers, acquaintances, friends... no one was immune from being a suspect. And Ted Bundy was in the mix; one of more than 3,000 possible suspects who was reported to the Seattle authorities. A former co-worker and professor from the University of Washington mentioned his name, as had one of Bundy's girlfriends.

Between February 1 and August 2, 1974, eight victims disappeared in Washington. On May 6, 1974, 22-year-old Roberta Kathleen Parks went missing in Oregon. Between October 2, 1974, and November 8, 1975, four teenagers between the ages of 16 and 17 disappeared in Utah. Between January and April 1975, three women disappeared from ski areas in Colorado. One body was recovered near Aspen, but the other two were never found. By July 1975, the focus was back on Utah when 21-year-old Nancy Baird disappeared from the town of Farmington. Once again, Utah authorities were faced with the absence of any evidence or a body.

In the early hours of August 16, 1975, Bundy was arrested in Granger, Utah, a suburb of Salt Lake City, after attempting to flee from a patrol car when officers tried to pull him over. Having eventually caught up with the 1968 tan VW Beetle, a search revealed a number of objects inside, including a crowbar stashed behind the driver's seat, a box of large green plastic rubbish bags, an ice pick, a flashlight, a pair of gloves, torn strips of sheeting, a knitted ski mask, a pair of handcuffs and a mask made from panty hose. None of the items, however, could be definitively linked to specific crimes, so Bundy was arrested on suspicion of burglary. The Seattle task force was informed that the Utah Sheriff's Office had Washington resident Theodore Robert Bundy in custody, and work began in earnest to link him to the Washington cases. Bundy remained calm during questioning, explaining that he needed the mask for skiing and had found the handcuffs in a dumpster. Utah detective Jerry Thompson connected Bundy and his Volkswagen to the DaRonch kidnapping and the missing girls and searched his apartment. That search uncovered a guide to Colorado ski resorts, a check mark by the Wildwood Inn where Caryn Campbell had disappeared, and a brochure advertising a Viewmont High School play in Bountiful, from where Debby Kent had disappeared. The police then brought Bundy in for a line-up before DaRonch and the Bountiful witnesses. They identified him as Officer Roseland, and as the man lurking about on the night Debby Kent disappeared. Bundy was sent to trial on February 23, 1976, and on March 1 was convicted of aggravated kidnapping, a first-degree felony, and was sentenced to one to 15 years in Utah State Prison. He would be eligible for parole in less than three years. With Colorado authorities still pursuing murder charges, Bundy was extradited there to stand trial.

On June 7, 1977, in preparation for a hearing in the Caryn Campbell murder trial, Bundy was taken to Pitkin County courthouse in Aspen. During a court recess, he was allowed to visit the courthouse's law library. There he jumped from a second-storey window and escaped, spraining his right ankle. He hobbled through the small town towards Aspen Mountain and made it to the top without being detected, where he rested for two days in an abandoned hunting cabin. However, he lost his sense of direction and wandered around the mountain, missing two trails that led down to the town of Crested Butte, his intended destination. At one point he talked his way out of danger after coming face-to-face with a gun-toting citizen who was one of the searchers scouring the mountain for him. On June 13, Bundy stole a Cadillac and drove into Aspen. He would have escaped but for two police deputies who noticed the weaving car with dimmed headlights. They pulled the vehicle over and recognised Bundy. He had been on the run for six days.

Back in custody, Bundy worked on a new escape plan. In jail at Glenwood Springs, Colorado, while awaiting trial, he acquired a hacksaw blade and $500 in cash. He later claimed that the blade came from another prison inmate. Over the next fortnight he managed to saw through the welds fixing a small metal plate in the ceiling of his cell and dieted to lose weight so he could fit through the hole and access the crawl space. An informant in the prison told officers how he had heard Bundy moving around the ceiling during the nights before his escape, but the matter was never investigated. When the Aspen trial judge ruled that the Caryn Campbell murder trial would start on January 9, 1978, and changed the venue to Colorado Springs, Bundy realised he had to escape before he was transferred out of Glenwood Springs. On December 30, 1977, he dressed warmly and packed books and files under his blanket to make it look like he was sleeping. Then he wriggled through the hole and made his way up into the crawl space before reaching a spot directly above the jailer's linen closet. Fortunately for him, the jailer and his wife were out for the evening. Bundy dropped down into the jailer's apartment and walked out the door.

He might well have been free, but Bundy had stepped out in the middle of a bitterly cold, snowy night. He managed to steal a broken-down MG, but once in the mountains the vehicle stalled. Stuck on the side of Interstate 70 in the middle of the night in a blizzard, another driver took pity on the escapee and gave him a ride into Vail. From there, Bundy caught a bus to Denver and boarded the TWA 8.55am flight to Chicago. The Glenwood Springs officers did not notice Bundy had escaped until noon on December 31, 1977. He had been gone for 17 hours. Eventually Bundy reached Tallahassee, Florida and, passing under the radar as Chris Hagan, he took up residence at the Oaks Apartment, 409 West College Avenue. On the night of January 14, 1978, he was observed by two co-eds who later testified to his 'unnerving' stare and unfriendly look. One of them actually danced with Bundy that same night, testifying that he looked 'like an ex-con' and that she was scared of him. By January 15, two more women were dead and another two severely assaulted. During the early hours of that day, Bundy entered Florida State University's Chi Omega sorority house, at 661 West Jefferson Street, Tallahassee, a few blocks from Bundy's apartment. He beat Margaret Bowman and Lisa Levy with a length of a tree branch used as a club and strangled them to death. Margaret's skull was crushed and literally laid open, and Bundy bit Lisa with sufficient intensity to be identified later as human bite marks (during the subsequent court case, the testimony of two forensic dental experts proved critical, when they testified that the imprints were Bundy's). Their housemates Kathy Kleiner and Karen Chandler sustained serious injuries. A resident returning home to the sorority house encountered Bundy as he was leaving, with a club in his hand. After about an hour, Bundy entered another home nearby and attacked student Cheryl Thomas, who survived. All five victims were repeatedly bludgeoned repeatedly with a blunt weapon.

On February 9, 12-year-old Kimberley Leach was kidnapped from junior high school in Lake City, Florida, and murdered. Two months later, after a major search, the girl's partially decomposed body was found in a wooded area near the Suwanee River. Two Lake City Holiday Inn employees and a handwriting expert established that Bundy had registered under another name at the Lake City Holiday Inn the day before her disappearance. A school crossing guard at the junior high school identified Bundy as leading a young girl to a van on the morning of the disappearance. Six days after her disappearance, Bundy was apprehended for a traffic violation. Officer David G. Lee, of the Penascola Police Department, had observed an orange Volkswagen at 1.30am on Cervantes Street. Making a U-turn to follow the car, he ran a tag on the vehicle, and it came back as having been stolen. With back-up units en route, Bundy tried to flee the scene but was apprehended after the officer fired a second shot. Once handcuffed and read his rights in the police vehicle, Bundy gave his name as Kenneth Miser. Bundy continued to use this false identity the following day, and insisted on calling Millard Farmer, a lawyer in Atlanta, who turned up late on the afternoon of February 16. Bundy was told he could use the telephone for two hours and call whomever he wanted, so long as he provided them with his real name, which he did. A short while later a Washington newspaper rang asking about Theodore Bundy, who was wanted for murder. Coincidentally, the FBI was contacted and told that one of their ten most wanted people was in custody. Bundy's identity was confirmed by a Penascola Police Department ID officer from an FBI flyer, and they learned that Bundy was wanted for escape and homicide in Colorado and was a suspect in 36 sex-related murders in the north-west United States.

On July 21, 1978, Bundy was indicted for the murder and kidnapping of Kimberly Leach. The trial was set in Suwanee County, Florida, for a later date and Bundy requested a change of venue, or in the alternative, abatement of prosecution. The latter motion was denied but the venue change was granted, and the case was transferred to the circuit court in Orange County, Orlando, Florida. On January 9, 1979, Hon. Edward D. Cowart was appointed to preside over the sorority house trial proceedings, with the first trial commencing and concluding on June 12, upon the granting of a change of venue from Tallahassee to Miami, Florida. The trial was then reset for June 25 in Miami. During the examination of jurors, about 24 were excused due to their knowledge of the case gained through pre-trial publicity. Once the trial began—the first on national television—the defence tactic was primarily an attack on the credibility and strength of the state's case. Bundy at first considered a plea deal for the Chi Omega killings, but later admitted that he never had any intention of pleading guilty. While his lawyer Michael Minerva was keen to withdraw from the case at this stage, the judge only allowed him to retreat to an advisory role, with Bundy serving as the head of his own defence. It is clear his hubris in thinking himself qualified to act as an attorney when he had not even finished law school would go on to cost him his life.

Erratic and impulsive, not only did Bundy battle with the prosecution, he often turned on his own public defenders. Nor was he adverse to grandstanding and making insignificant requests before the judge. At one point, according to prosecutor Larry Simpson, he even filed a motion for a change of menu because he was sick of eating grilled cheese sandwiches. He took a kind of sick pleasure in cross-examining first responders about his crime scenes. It was all to no avail, as he was found guilty on all counts and sentenced to death in both trials. The defence then moved for the imposition of life sentences based on an aborted plea agreement. The defence theory was that the defendant, by not pleading guilty and insisting on a trial by jury, was being punished for the exercise of this constitutional right. The motion was denied. The court found the capital felonies to have been committed while Bundy was engaged in the crime of burglary, and that the capital crimes were especially heinous, atrocious or cruel, and followed the jury advisory sentence of death. Bundy was sentenced to die in the electric chair for the sorority house murders of Margaret Bowman and Lisa Levy.

A documented report of one of the Chi Omega sorority members, Nita Neary, had seen a man walk down the stairs on the night of the murders, and her testimony was used during Bundy's trial. 'She was able to give a good, strong description,' commented lead prosecutor Larry Simpson. 'Nita Neary did meet with an artist and drew a sketch of the person that she saw leaving the Chi Omega house… it looked like Mr. Bundy.' However, it was not merely a passing similarity based on eyewitness reports that swayed the trial in the prosecution's favour. Bundy's hair matched fibres found in a pantyhose mask, and the infamous bite mark left on Lisa Levy—a pivotal scene in a later Netflix movie—was also strong evidence against the killer. 'I think the bite mark itself is indicative of the primal rage that Mr. Bundy must have been in at the time that he committed those murders,' said Simpson. 'It was just a total homicidal rage. I thought a lot about the parents of the girls that were killed during the prosecution of this case. It's one of the things that kept me going.'

In January 1980, Bundy was back in court, this time standing trial in Orlando where he was convicted and sentenced to death for the kidnap and first-degree murder of Kimberly Leach. Bundy was determined to handle his own defence and wavered his constitutional right to representation. During the trial, Bundy took advantage of an old law still on the books in the state of Florida that allowed a 'declaration' in court to constitute a legal marriage. Bundy proposed to former co-worker Carole Ann Boone, who had moved to Florida to be near Bundy, while questioning her on the stand. She readily accepted and Bundy announced to the courtroom that they were married. Following numerous conjugal visits between Bundy and his new wife, Boone gave birth to a daughter in October 1982. However, in 1986 Boone moved back to Washington and never returned to Florida.

On February 7 at the Old Orange County Courthouse, Bundy was convicted on all counts, principally due to fibres found in his van that matched Leach's clothing and an eye-witness who saw him leading Leach away. The jury recommended death and Bundy was subsequently sentenced to a term of life imprisonment. The Governor of Florida signed a death warrant scheduling Bundy's execution for November 18, 1986. Eventually convicted of just three killings in two separate Florida trials, Bundy spent nine years on death row, before eventually exhausting his appeals. The final convictions ultimately convinced him to confess, admitting to a staggering 30 murders.

While awaiting execution in Starke Prison, Bundy was housed in the cell next to serial killer and cannibal Ottis Toole. Born on March 5, 1947, in Jacksonville, Florida, Toole committed his first murder at the age of 14. He began a sexual and criminal relationship with Henry Lee Lucas in the 1970s. After their arrest, the pair confessed to more than 100 murders, including killing *America's Most Wanted* host John Walsh's son. Toole died in prison in 1996. FBI profiler Robert Ressler met with Bundy as part of his work interviewing serial killers, and found him to be uncooperative and manipulative, willing to speak only in the third person and only in hypothetical terms. Writing in 1992, Ressler spoke of his impression of Bundy in comparison to other serial killers:

'This guy was an animal, and it amazed me that the media seemed unable to understand that.' During the same period, Special Agent William Hagmaier, of the Federal Bureau of Investigation's Behavioural Sciences Unit, often visited Bundy. Eventually Bundy confessed to Hagmaier many details of the murders that had until then been unknown or unconfirmed. In October 1984, Bundy contacted former King County homicide detective Bob Keppel and offered to assist the ongoing search for the Green River Killer by providing his own insights and analysis. The Green River Killer, Gary Leon Ridgway, murdered at least 49 women in Washington State before he was caught in 2001. Keppel and Green River Task Force detective Dave Reichert travelled to Florida to interview Bundy. Both detectives later stated that the interviews were of little help to the investigation but provided a greater insight into Bundy's own mind.

Bundy contacted Keppel again in 1988. By this point, his appeals were exhausted. He had beaten previous death warrants for March 4, July 2 and November 18, 1986. With execution imminent, he confessed to eight unsolved murders in Washington State for which he was the prime suspect. Bundy told Keppel he left five bodies on Taylor Mountain, not four as originally thought. He also confessed in detail to the murder of Georgeann Hawkins, describing how he lured her to his car, clubbed her with a tyre iron he'd stashed on the ground under his car, drove away and later raped and strangled her. After the interview, Keppel reported being shocked, and that Bundy was the kind of man who was 'born to kill'. Keppel stated: 'He is just totally consumed with murder all the time.' Bundy had hoped he could use the revelations and partial confessions to get another stay of execution or possibly commute his sentence to life imprisonment. At one point, a legal advocate working for Bundy asked many of the families of the victims to fax letters to Florida Governor Robert Martinez and ask for mercy for Bundy to find out where the remains of their loved ones were. All the families refused. The night before his execution, Bundy granted a taped interview to James Dobson, the psychologist and founder of the Christian evangelical organisation Focus on the Family. Bundy stated that while pornography did not cause him to commit murder, the consumption of violent pornography helped 'shape and mould' his violence into 'behaviour too terrible to describe'. He said: 'You are going to kill me, and that will protect society from me. But out there are many, many more people who are addicted to pornography, and you are doing nothing about that.'

The life and crimes of Ted Bundy were recently chronicled in Netflix's *Extremely Wicked, Shockingly Evil and Vile*. The film mainly explored Bundy's relationship with his former girlfriend, Elizabeth Kloepfer, and was based on her own memoir published under the pseudonym Elizabeth Kendall, which ends shortly before Bundy's execution in 1989. The film took some liberties with the facts, including Kloepfer visiting him in Florida State Prison just days before his execution and finally learning the truth. According to the film website Oxygen, that emotional catharsis happened years earlier over the phone. 'The force would just consume me,' he told her. 'Like one night, I was walking by the campus and I followed this sorority girl. I didn't want to follow her. I didn't do anything but follow her and that's how it was. I'd be out late at night and follow people like that… I'd try not to, but I'd do it anyway.' When Bundy contacted Kloepfer shortly after his arrest in Florida, he was in tears. According to her memoir, he was desperate to take responsibility for his actions. When he admitted his violent deeds, she replied by saying 'I love you.' She wasn't sure how else to respond. 'I tried to suppress it,' he told her, 'it was taking more and more of my time. That's why I didn't do well in school. My time was being used trying to make my life look normal. But I wasn't normal.'

There is no definitive agreement on when and where Bundy began killing. Ann Rule and former King County detective Robert D. Keppel, who investigated the 1974 Washington murders, believe Bundy may have started as far back as his early teens. While Bundy's first known victim was killed in 1974, one of his possible earlier murders was that of Ann Marie Burr. The eight-year-old disappeared from her Tacoma home in the middle of the night on August 31, 1961. At the time, 14-year-old Bundy, lived a few miles away. Among the few clues at the property was an open window, a footprint and an unlocked front door. Ann Marie's parents and sister were in the house when she disappeared. Bundy denied responsibility, even when the child's mother wrote to him prior to his execution asking for closure. In 2011, existing evidence did not contain enough amplifiable DNA to be compared to Bundy's profile.

Ted Bundy did not fit the stereotype of a murderer, yet he was responsible for one of the most gruesome and notorious killing sprees in American history. He was never tried for most of his crimes. However, he did make one final effort to trade information on an additional 50 murders of which he had knowledge in exchange for a stay of execution. His appeals exhausted, he was electrocuted on January 24, 1989, at the Florida State Prison in Starke. According to the LA Times, reporting from inside the prison, there were 42 witnesses. Superintendent Tom Barton asked Bundy whether he had any last words. 'I'd like to give my love to my family and friends,' he said, before a strap was pulled across his mouth and chin and the metal skullcap bolted in place, its heavy black veil covering his face. Two thousand volts surged through the wires and 60 seconds later, the machine was turned off. At 7.16am, Ted Bundy was dead. Those several hundred people gathered outside the prison cheered.

After his brain was removed in the name of science, Bundy's body was cremated and his ashes scattered in Washington's Cascade Mountains, as he'd requested. The final irony: it was in this very mountain range that Bundy dumped at least four of his murder victims.

CHAPTER 3

JOHN WAYNE GACY

THE KILLER CLOWN

'Clowns can get away with murder.'—John Wayne Gacy.

THE CAMBRIDGE English Dictionary describes a clown as 'an entertainer who wears funny clothes, has a painted face, and makes people laugh by performing tricks and behaving in a silly way'. As children we laughed at their daft antics or were frightened by their exaggerated make-up. It is a little-known fact that all clowns can be traced back to one of three types: the Whiteface, the Tramp, and the Auguste (or fool). Each type has its own history, its own set of clown characteristics, and a typical look. But there was another clown altogether. One who dressed to thrill... and kill.

John Wayne Gacy was born on March 17, 1942, in Chicago, Illinois. His father, John Stanley Gacy, a First World War veteran of Polish descent, was an auto repair mechanic. His mother, Marion Elaine Robinson, was of English and Danish descent. John's sisters, Joanne and Karen, were born in 1939 and 1944. His father was an alcoholic and referred to his son as 'sissy', or 'dumb' and 'stupid', belittling him and comparing him unfavourably to his sisters. Young Gacy and his siblings would often feel the brunt of their father's anger, enduring abuse and beatings with a razor strap. One of his earliest childhood memories was of being beaten for accidentally disarranging car engine components his father had assembled. He was just four years old. On another occasion, Gacy was knocked unconscious after being struck across the head with a broomstick. The children's mother, who called her son Johnny, also suffered at the hands of her husband. She would try and protect them from the violent outbursts. Karen later said they learned to toughen up against the beatings, and that Gacy would not cry.

Home life was a challenge, and so was school for Gacy, where he suffered further alienation. He was unable to play with other children due to a congenital heart condition, and his ailment was looked upon by his father as yet another failing. A high school friends recalled several instances in which Gacy Senior ridiculed or beat his son without provocation. In 1957, the same friend witnessed an incident at the Gacy household, when Gacy's father shouted and hit him for no reason. Gacy simply 'put up his hands to defend himself', adding that he never fought back. Aged 18, in 1960 Gacy worked as an assistant precinct captain for a Democratic

Party candidate in his neighbourhood. The position earned him more criticism from his father, who accused his son of being a 'patsy'. That year, Gacy Senior bought him a car, keeping it in his name until his son completed the monthly payments. This took several years, and whenever Gacy did not do as his father said, he confiscated the keys. In 1962, Gacy bought an extra set of keys. In response, his father removed the vehicle's distributor cap and held on to it for three days. Once he had the car running again, Gacy left the family home and headed west for the bright lights of Las Vegas. With no money to speak of, he applied for a job as an ambulance driver at the Palm Mortuary Memorial Park, having lied about his age (the minimum age being 21). When his employers discovered the truth, they offered him alternative employment as a mortuary assistant. The work saw him moving corpses and material from the hospital to the funeral home. Still short of money, he was allowed to sleep in the premises, and would bed down on a cot adjacent to the embalming room. Alone at night, he would pull out the drawers and examine the bodies, talking to them, undressing them, and neatly folding their clothes next to the caskets. Gacy later confessed that on one evening, he clambered into the coffin of a deceased teenage male and embraced and caressed the body before experiencing a sense of shock. The macabre incidents prompted the director of the funeral home to call the police and although they could not identify Gacy as the culprit, he quit three months later and returned home to Chicago.

Despite that he'd failed to graduate from high school, Gacy enrolled at Northwestern Business College in Bridgeview, Illinois, and graduated in 1963. He embarked on a management trainee position with the Nunn-Bush Shoe Company and in 1964 was transferred to Springfield, Illinois, first as a salesman and then department manager. It was there that he met and began courting co-worker Marlynn Myers. During this time, Gacy joined the Springfield Jaycees, working tirelessly for the organisation and being named Key Man in April 1964. By the following year Gacy had risen to the position of vice president and was named as the third most outstanding Jaycee within the state.

After a nine-month courtship, Gacy and Marlynn married and relocated to Iowa, where Gacy took over the management of his father-in-law's three Kentucky Fried Chicken restaurants in Waterloo. The understanding was that the newlyweds would move into Marlynn's parents' home, which was vacated for them. There, the happy couple started a family. They had two children, Michael and Christine, and Gacy would later describe this period of his life as 'perfect', adding that he finally earned the long-sought approval of his father. But there was a seedier side to his life, involving wife-swapping, prostitution, pornography and drug use. He opened a club in the basement of the family home, where he allowed young male employees of his restaurants to drink alcohol and play pool. Gacy would make sexual advances toward them and if rebuffed, he would claim they were jokes or a test of morals.

In May 1968 Gacy was indicted by a grand jury in Black Hawk County for allegedly committing the act of sodomy with teenager Donald Voorhees. At first Gacy denied the charges and demanded to take a polygraph test, which indicated that Gacy was nervous when denying wrongdoing. Gacy also insisted that the charges against him were politically motivated, stating that the boy's father had opposed his nomination for appointment as president of the Iowa Jaycees. Several fellow Jaycees found Gacy's story credible and rallied to support him. On August 30, Gacy persuaded one of his employees, 18-year-old Russell Schroeder, to physically assault Voorhees to discourage him from testifying the upcoming trial. The boy was lured to a secluded spot, Mace was sprayed in his face and he was beaten. He escaped and immediately reported the assault to the police, identifying his attacker. Schroeder was arrested the following day and confessed. Gacy was arrested and additionally charged for hiring Schroeder to assault and intimidate Voorhees. On September 12, Gacy was ordered to undergo evaluation at the Psychiatric Hospital of the State University of Iowa. Two doctors examined him over 17 days before concluding he had an antisocial personality disorder incorporating constructs such as sociopathy and psychopathy. They said he was unlikely to benefit from therapy or medical treatment, and that his behaviour pattern was likely to bring him into repeated conflict with society. The doctors also concluded he was mentally competent to stand trial. A section of the report detailing Gacy's 1968 psychiatric evaluation stated: 'The most striking aspect of the test results is the patient's total denial of responsibility for everything that has happened to him. He can produce an alibi for everything. He presents himself as a victim of circumstances and blames other people who are out to get him… the patient attempts to assure a sympathetic response by depicting himself as being at the mercy of a hostile environment.' At a formal arraignment on November 7, 1968, Gacy entered a plea of guilty to one count of sodomy in relation to the charges filed against him by Donald Voorhees, and a plea of not guilty to the other charges lodged against him by other youths. Despite his lawyers' recommendations for probation, on December 3, 1968, Gacy was convicted of sodomy and sentenced to 10 years' confinement in the Iowa State Men's Reformatory (Anamosa State Penitentiary). On the same day, his wife petitioned for divorce, requesting possession of the couple's home, property, sole custody of their two children and subsequent alimony payments. The court ruled in her favour and the divorce was finalised on September 18, 1969. Gacy would never see his first wife or children again.

He proved to be a model prisoner and quickly rose to become head cook. He also secured an increase in the inmates' daily pay in the prison mess hall and supervised several projects to improve conditions, including overseeing the installation of a miniature golf course in the recreation yard. In June 1969, he applied to the State of Iowa Board of Parole for early release, but the application was denied. In preparation for a second scheduled parole hearing in May the following year, Gacy completed 16 high school courses and obtained his diploma in the November. On Christmas Day 1969, his father died from cirrhosis of the liver. Gacy was not informed until two days later, when he was said to have collapsed to the floor, sobbing uncontrollably, and had to be supported by prison staff. Gacy then requested supervised compassionate leave from prison to attend the funeral in Chicago. His request was denied.

On June 18, 1970, Gacy was granted parole with 12 months' probation, after serving 18 months of his 10-year sentence. The parole came with two conditions: he had to relocate to Chicago to live with his mother and observe a 10pm curfew, with the Iowa Board of Parole receiving regular updates as to his progress. Within 24 hours of his release, he was home, and soon picked up a job as a short-order cook in a restaurant. On February 12, 1971, Gacy was charged with sexual misconduct towards a young male. The youth claimed Gacy had lured him into his car at Chicago's Greyhound bus terminal and driven him to his home, where he had attempted to force the youth into sex. The complaint was subsequently dismissed when the youth failed to appear in court. While the incident violated the conditions of his parole, the Iowa Board of Parole did not learn of it and eight months later, Gacy's parole ended, and he began life anew. With financial assistance from his mother, he bought a house at 8213 West Summerdale Avenue in Norwood Park Township, an unincorporated area of Cook County. He was courting Carole Hoff, a divorcee with two young daughters. The couple had briefly dated in high school, and she had been a friend of his younger sister. They became engaged and Carole moved in, and shortly before their wedding on July 1, 1972, Gacy's mother moved out. A week before the nuptials, on June 22, he was arrested and charged with aggravated battery and reckless conduct. A complaint had been filed by a youth named Jackie Dee, who said Gacy impersonated a police officer, flashing a sheriff's badge, lured him into his car and forced him to perform oral sex. The charges were later dropped after the Dee attempted to blackmail Gacy into paying money in exchange for dropping the charges.

With his new wife and stepdaughters settled into 8213 West Summerdale Avenue, Gacy quit his job at the restaurant and started a construction business called PDM Contractors (PDM being the initials for painting, decorating and maintenance), carrying out minor repair work, such as sign-writing, pouring concrete and redecorating. The firm later expanded to include projects such as interior design remodelling, installation, assembly, and landscaping, and by 1978 PDM had an annual turnover of more than $200,000. In 1973, Gacy and a teenage employee went to Florida to view a property Gacy had purchased. Gacy raped the youth in their hotel room. When they returned to Chicago, the victim drove to Gacy's house and beat him. Gacy's mother-in-law intervened and he told his wife that the youth was angry because he'd refused to pay him for poor quality work. By now Gacy was popular among his neighbours and colleagues, who thought him gregarious and helpful. He had also become active in Democratic Party politics, offering the labour of his company employees for free. Gacy was rewarded by being appointed to serve upon the Norwood Park Township street lighting committee, and subsequently earned the title of precinct captain. In 1975, he was appointed director of Chicago's annual Polish Constitution Day Parade and supervised the annual event from 1975 until 1978. Through this work, he met and was photographed with then First Lady Rosalynn Carter, wife of former President Jimmy Carter.

In 1974 Gacy began to host annual summer parties. He had also become aware of a Jolly Joker clown club, whose members would regularly perform at fundraising events and parades, and voluntarily entertain children in hospital. In late 1975, Gacy joined the Jolly Jokers and created his own performance characters, Pogo the Clown and Patches the Clown. Having designed his own costumes and taught himself how to apply make-up, he began appearing at children's parties and charity shows. It was his habit of wearing the costume at such events that later would lead to him being nicknamed the Killer Clown. He was also known on several occasions to arrive at his favourite drinking venue, The Good Luck Lounge, still in his outfit, having performed at an event and stopping for a sociable drink before going home. By now though, Gacy's home life was unravelling. After he and his wife had sex on Mother's Day 1975, he informed Carole he was bisexual, and they would no longer sleep together. He spent most evenings away from home, returning in the early hours with the excuse of working late. Carole later claimed he brought young men and boys home to the garage, and that she discovered a stash of homosexual pornography. The couple divorced by mutual consent in March 1976.

Unbeknown to family, friends, colleagues and employees, the affable businessman and community worker was also a murderer—and had been since January 1972. Timothy Jack McCoy was 15 years old when Gacy met him outside the city's Greyhound bus terminal in downtown Chicago. After showing the boy around the city, Gacy offered him a safe space to sleep overnight with the guarantee that he would return him in time to catch his bus. According to Tim Cahill in his 1986 book, Buried Dreams: Inside the Mind of a Serial Killer, McCoy was cooking eggs and cutting a slab of bacon when he went to wake his host. Gacy awoke to the sight of McCoy still holding the kitchen knife and reacted violently, wrestling the knife from the boy's hand before slamming his head against the bedroom wall. He then kicked McCoy and stabbed him twice in the chest, killing him. The murder resulted in Gacy experiencing an orgasm, and he later said it triggered an association in his mind between murder and ecstasy. 'That's when I realised that death was the ultimate thrill,' he said. He buried McCoy in the crawl space of his house and later covered the youth's grave with a layer of concrete. This was the only murder in which Gacy used a knife. His other victims died of strangulation with a rope or board. According to Gacy, the second time he killed was around January 1974. The victim was an unidentified teenage youth between the age of 14 and 18 with medium brown hair, whom Gacy strangled before stowing the youth's body in his closet prior to burial. Gacy said fluid leaked out of the youth's mouth and nose while he was stored, staining the carpet. As a result, Gacy would stuff cloth rags or the victims' own underwear in their mouths to prevent a recurrence. This unidentified victim was buried about 15ft from the barbecue pit in Gacy's backyard.

By 1975, PDM Contractors was thriving and Gacy found himself working up to 16-hour days to fulfil agreed commitments with clients. He also began to increase the frequency of his excursions for sex with young males and would often refer to these jaunts between the years 1976 and 1978 as the 'cruising years'. With his home all to himself, he was free to hunt for victims and bring them home at any time of the day or night. In May 1975, Gacy hired 15-year-old Anthony Antonucci, one of many high school students and young men he employed. Two months later, Gacy went to the youth's home while he was alone; Antonucci had injured his foot at work. Gacy plied him with alcohol, wrestled him to the floor and cuffed his hands behind his back. The cuff on his right wrist was loose, however, and Antonucci freed his arm after Gacy left the room. When his employer returned, Antonucci, who was a member of his high school wrestling team, wrestled Gacy to the floor, got hold of the handcuff key and cuffed Gacy's own hands behind his back.

Screaming various threats, Gacy calmed down and promised to leave if Antonucci removed the handcuffs. He agreed and Gacy left the house. Antonucci would later recall Gacy telling him as he lay on the floor: 'Not only are you the only one who got out of the cuffs; you got them on me.' A week after the attempted assault, on July 31, John Butkovich, another of Gacy's employees, disappeared. The day before, 18-year-old Butkovich had threatened Gacy about two weeks' outstanding back pay. Gacy lured Butkovich to his home while his wife and stepchildren were visiting his sister in Arkansas, on the pretence of settling the issue. After conning the youth into allowing his wrists to be cuffed behind his back, Gacy strangled him to death and buried his body under the concrete floor of his garage. Gacy admitted to having 'sat on the kid's chest for a while' before killing him. Butkovich's father contacted Gacy, who said he was happy to help with the search and was sorry he'd 'run away'. When questioned about the disappearance, Gacy admitted that Butkovich and two friends had arrived at his home demanding the overdue pay but claimed all three had left after a compromise was reached. Butkovich's parents called police more than 100 times over the following three years, urging them to investigate Gacy further.

Using his outgoing personality to his best advantage, smooth-talking Gacy lured dozens of young males to his home, where he would torture, rape and kill them. Chicago, however, was slow to catch on to the disappearance of dozens of young men and boys. His modus operandi was to drive around Chicago seeking young male runaways, former cons or male prostitutes. His victims ranged in age from nine to 20. Pretending to be an officer of the law, Gacy would flash a badge or a gun and then arrest them. He would befriend them and take them to his home, showing them tricks with 'magic handcuffs'. Once he had subdued his victims he would torture, sodomise and garrotte them, before burying them in the crawl space. With so many murders and so many bodies to dispose of, Gacy soon ran out of space so he decided to dispose of his last four victims in the nearby Des Plaines River via the I-55 bridge.

The majority of Gacy's murders were committed between 1976 and 1978. A month after his divorce was finalised, he abducted and murdered 18-year-old Darrell Samson. The victim was last been seen alive in Chicago on April 6, 1976. Five weeks later, on the afternoon of May 14, 15-year-old Randall Reffett disappeared while walking home from Senn High School. He was gagged with a cloth, causing him to die of asphyxiation. Hours after Reffett had been abducted, 14-year-old Samuel Stapleton vanished as he walked to his home from his sister's apartment. Both youths were buried in the same grave in the crawl space of Gacy's home. On December 30, 1977, Gacy abducted 19-year-old student Robert Donnelly at gunpoint from a Chicago bus stop. He drove Donnelly home, raped and tortured him with various devices, and repeatedly dunked his head into a bathtub filled with water until he passed out, then revived him. Donnelly later testified that he was in such pain that he asked Gacy to kill him to 'get it over with', to which Gacy replied: 'I'm getting round to it.' Gacy drove Donnelly to his workplace, removed the handcuffs and released him. Donnelly reported the assault and Gacy was questioned by the authorities on January 6, 1978. He admitted to having had 'slave-sex' with Donnelly but insisted everything was consensual. The Police believed him, and no charges were brought. A month later, Gacy killed 19-year-old William Kindred. He had disappeared on February 16, 1978, having told his fiancée that he was spending the evening in a bar. Kindred was the final victim to be buried in Gacy's crawl space. It was then that he switched to disposing of his victims in the Des Plaines River.

In March 1978, Gacy lured 26-year-old Jeffrey Rignall into his car. He was then chloroformed before being driven to Gacy's house on Summerdale, where he was raped, tortured with instruments including lit candles and whips, and repeatedly chloroformed into unconsciousness. Gacy then drove his victim to Lincoln Park and dumped him there. Rignall was unconscious but still breathing and managed to stagger to his girlfriend's apartment. The police were again informed of the assault but did not investigate Gacy. Rignall, however, was able to recall Gacy's distinctive black Oldsmobile, the Kennedy Expressway and particular side streets and, as a result, he staked out the exit on the Expressway where he knew he had been driven until he saw the vehicle. Rignall and his friends followed the vehicle to 8213 West Summerdale and Gacy was arrested. He was facing an impending trial for a battery charge for the Rignall incident when he was eventually arrested in December for the murders. His final act of violence occurred two months before, on October 12, 1978. Fifteen-year-old Robert Piest told his mother he was going for a job interview with Gacy, and that was the last she heard from him. Worried, she contacted the police. Des Pleines officers called at Gacy's home, noticed the odour emanating from the crawl space and immediately obtained search warrants. It proved to be a real-life chamber of horrors as 28 bodies were discovered under the house and buried in the backyard. 'Gacy was just pure evil,' said former Des Plaines officer Mike Albrecht. 'He was just an evil, evil man.'

By December 16, Gacy was still denying that he had anything to do with Piest's disappearance and accused surveillance officers of harassing him because of his political connections and his use of recreational drugs. Knowing these officers were unlikely to arrest him on anything trivial, he openly taunted them by flouting traffic laws and succeeded in losing his pursuers on more than one occasion. On December 17, a further examination of Gacy's Oldsmobile was conducted, and investigators discovered a small cluster of fibres, which were sent for further analysis. That evening, officers used three trained German Shepherd search dogs to determine whether Piest had been present in any of Gacy's vehicles. One dog approached the Oldsmobile and lay on the passenger seat. The handler said this was a 'death reaction'. That same evening, Gacy invited two of the surveillance detectives to a restaurant for a meal. In the early hours of the following day, he invited the same officers to another restaurant where, over breakfast, he talked of his business, his marriages and his activities as a registered clown. During this conversation, Gacy remarked: 'You know… clowns can get away with murder.' That afternoon, he drove to his lawyers' office to prepare a $750,000 civil suit against the Des Plaines police, demanding that they cease their surveillance. At the same time, a serial number of a Nisson Pharmacy photo receipt found in Gacy's kitchen was traced to 17-year-old Kim Byers, a colleague of Piest at Nisson Pharmacy, who said she'd placed it in the pocket of a parka which she gave to Piest as he was leaving the store to talk with a contractor. This revelation contradicted Gacy's previous statements that he had had no contact with Robert Piest on the evening of December 11.

On December 19, investigators began compiling evidence for a second search warrant of Gacy's house. That same day, Gacy's lawyers filed the civil suit against the Des Plaines police and a hearing was scheduled for December 22. That afternoon, Gacy invited two of the surveillance detectives inside his house. As one officer distracted him with conversation, another officer went into Gacy's bedroom in an unsuccessful attempt to write down the serial number of the Motorola TV set they suspected belonged to another victim. While flushing Gacy's toilet, the officer noticed a smell emanating from a heating duct he suspected could be that of rotting corpses. Gacy's house in Norwood Park lay just east of Chicago's busy O'Hare International Airport.

Situated in a pleasant middle-class neighbourhood, he had outfitted the simple one-storey ranch house with a trap door leading to a crawl space beneath the house. The unusual smell had not previously gone unnoticed by family members or visitors, but Gacy had always passed it off as mould or rodents. As planes screamed daily overhead from O'Hare, young boys' screams went unanswered far below.

With Gacy under arrest, the house was dismantled in a hunt for evidence. On the evening of December 20, Gacy attended a pre-scheduled meeting at the offices of his lawyers in Park Ridge, with a view to discussing the progress of his civil suit. Having been asked by Sam Amirante what he had to discuss with them, Gacy picked up a copy of the Daily Herald that was lying on a desk, pointed to a front page article covering the disappearance of Robert Piest and informed his lawyers: 'This boy is dead. He's in a river.' He then said he had 'been the judge… jury and executioner of many, many people'. Between December 22 and 29, 1978, a total of 27 bodies were recovered from Gacy's property, 26 of which were buried in the crawl space. John Butkovich's body was found buried beneath the concrete floor of the garage, precisely where Gacy had marked the youth's grave with a can of spray paint.

After being informed that he would face murder charges, Gacy told officers he wanted to 'clear the air'. In the early hours of December 22, he finally confessed to killing at least 30 people. He would target Caucasian male runaways or male prostitutes in their mid-teens to early twenties from the Chicago Greyhound bus station or off the streets. He would take them to his house by promising them money for sex, offering them a job, simply grabbing them or forcing them into his car at gunpoint. At his home, he would handcuff or tie them up after intoxicating them with alcohol or knocking them out with chloroform. He would torture them in various ways, such as using a fire poker, dripping hot melted candle wax on their bodies, repeatedly drowning them in his bathtub or by placing them on a homemade 'rack'. As a show of dominance, he would urinate on his victims and rape them, both before and after killing them. One of his most infamous ways of binding his victims was convincing them to allow him to handcuff them under the pretence of a magic trick. Gacy would often stick paper towels or clothing, such as a sock or their own underwear in their mouths to muffle their screams, causing them to fatally asphyxiate. He would also kill by strangling them with a rope or a board as he sexually assaulted them with sex toys, before burying the bodies. Periodically, Gacy would pour lime in the crawl space to hasten decomposition. He had planned to conceal the bodies by covering the entire space with concrete and, having lost count of the number of victims buried there, considered stowing bodies in his attic, instead choosing the Des Plaines River.

In January 1979, severe snowfall hampered excavations at the house, and it was not until March that they resumed. All the while, Gacy insisted that the remains of all his victims had been found. On March 9, the body of a 28th victim was discovered buried in a pit close to a barbecue grill in the back yard. Several plastic bags had been used to wrap it up. There was a silver ring on the fourth finger of the left hand, indicating that the male victim had been married. A week later, another victim was found buried beneath the joists of the dining room floor. Three bodies found in the nearby Des Plaines River between June and December 1978 were also confirmed to have been Gacy's victims. One was discovered entangled in exposed roots on the edge of the river in Grundy County, and dental records revealed it was Robert Piest. An autopsy showed that he'd died from suffocation after three wads of 'paper-like material' had been shoved down his throat. The following year, in April 1979, Gacy's house and all structures on the land were demolished, and a new house was eventually built. According to one worker involved in the demolition, 'if the devil's alive, he lived here.'

At the request of his defence counsel, Gacy spent more than 300 hours in the year before his trial with doctors at the Menard Correctional Centre, where he underwent a variety of psychological tests before a panel of psychiatrists to determine whether he was mentally competent to stand trial. Charged with 33 murders, the trial began on February 6, 1980, in Cook County, Illinois, before Judge Louis Garippo and a jury selected from Rockford. Having previously confessed to the crimes, the arguments were focused on whether Gacy could be declared insane and remitted to a state mental facility. Gacy claimed he had multiple personalities and one in particular, Jack, was evil.

Defence attorneys convinced him to plead not guilty by way of insanity, however, the disturbing testimony of some of his surviving victims and of employees who were involved in the grave digging showed well-planned pre-meditation. Psychiatric evaluation proved the claim to be false. During the fifth week of the trial, Gacy wrote a letter to Judge Garippo requesting a mistrial on a number of bases. He did not approve of his lawyers' insanity plea approach, and desired to take to the stand but his lawyers had not allowed it. He also said his defence team had not called enough witnesses and that the police were lying about statements he had purportedly made to detectives after his arrest. Judge Garippo addressed Gacy's letter by informing him that, under law, he had the choice to testify.

On March 11, final arguments from both prosecution and defence attorneys began, and concluded the following day. Prosecuting attorney Terry Sullivan argued first, referring to Gacy as the 'worst of all murderers.' 'John Gacy has accounted for more human devastation than many earthly catastrophes, but one must tremble,' he said. 'I tremble when thinking about just how close he came to getting away with it all.' Defence counsel Sam Amirante portrayed Gacy as a 'man driven by compulsions he was unable to control', urging the jury to put aside any prejudice and deliver a verdict of not guilty by reason of insanity. The psychology of Gacy's behavior, he added, would be of benefit to scientific research and that the psychology of his mind should be studied. The following morning prosecutor William Kunkle referred to the defence's contention of insanity as 'a sham', bristling at pleas for mercy and arguing that the facts of the case demonstrated Gacy's ability to think logically and control his actions. Kunkle also referred to the testimony of a doctor who examined Gacy in 1968 and diagnosed him as an anti-social personality, capable of committing crimes without remorse. Kunkle indicated that had the recommendations of this doctor been heeded, Gacy would have not been freed. During his own summation for the jury, Kunkle tore down the 22 photographs of the known victims and strode to a spot in the courtroom where the trap door to Gacy's crawl space was on display. 'You want to show this man mercy?' asked Kunkle to the jury. 'You show him the same mercy he showed when he took these innocent lives off the face of the earth and put them here!' Kunkle then hurled the victims' photographs through the trap door. The images hit the front of the jury box and scattered on the floor. 'It was the best pin-drop moment I've ever had,' said Kunkle later.

On March 12, 1980, the jury took one hour and 45 minutes to find Gacy guilty of 33 counts of murder. He was also found guilty of one count of sexual assault and one count of indecent liberties with a child. The following day, the prosecution requested a death sentence for each murder committed after the Illinois statute on capital punishment came into effect in June 1977. The defence requested life imprisonment. The judge sentenced Gacy to the death penalty for 12 counts and life imprisonment for 21 counts, and an initial date of execution was set for June 2, 1980. Gacy spent the next 14 years on death row at Menard Correctional Centre in Illinois, from where he read law books and filed multiple motions and appeals relating to issues such as the validity of the first search warrant granted to Des Plaines police and his objection to his lawyers' insanity plea defence at his trial. Gacy contended that, although he held 'some knowledge' of five of the murders, the other 28 murders had been committed by employees who were in possession of keys to his house while he was away on business trips. On February 15, 1983, Gacy was attacked by fellow death row inmate Henry Brisbon, known as the I-57 killer. Gacy was participating in a voluntary work programme when Brisbon ran towards him and stabbed him once in the upper arm with a sharpened wire. In mid-1984, the Supreme Court of Illinois upheld Gacy's conviction and ordered that he be executed by lethal injection on November 14. He filed an appeal against the decision, which was denied by the Supreme Court on March 4, 1985. In May 1986, the ninth victim exhumed from the crawl space was identified as Timothy Jack McCoy, Gacy's first victim. Another victim was identified in November 2011 through DNA testing as William George Bundy, a 19-year-old construction worker who'd apparently worked for Gacy. He was last seen by his family on his way to a party on October 26, 1976. During 1986, Gacy filed a further post-conviction petition, seeking a new trial. His then defence lawyer, Richard Kling, argued that Gacy had been provided with ineffective legal counsel at the 1980 trial. The petition was dismissed on September 11,

1986. In 1992 the television film To Catch a Killer, starring Brian Dennehy as Gacy, Michael Riley and Margot Kidder, explored the efforts made to find out what happened to missing teenage boys later discovered to be among Gacy's victims. The film was nominated for an Emmy for Dennehy's performance. Gacy wrote to him from prison, protesting his portrayal in the film and proclaiming his innocence.

On the morning of May 9, 1994, Gacy was transferred from the Menard Correctional Centre to Stateville Correctional Centre in Crest Hill to be executed. That afternoon, he was allowed a private picnic in the prison grounds with his family. He ate a dozen fried shrimp, a bucket of Kentucky Fried Chicken and French fries, fresh strawberries, and a Diet Coke. In the hours leading up to the execution, a crowd of more than 1,000 people gathered outside, among them a minority group of anti-death penalty protesters. Some of those in favour of the execution wore T-shirts depicting Gacy's previous community services as a clown and bearing satirical slogans such as 'no tears for the clown'. By stark contrast, the protesters observed a silent candlelight vigil. That evening, Gacy observed prayer with a Catholic priest before being escorted to the Stateville execution chamber to receive a lethal injection. But before Gacy's execution began, the potassium chloride used to perform the execution unexpectedly solidified, clogging the IV tube administering the chemicals into Gacy's arm. Blinds covering the window through which witnesses observed the execution were drawn, and the tube was replaced. After 10 minutes, the blinds were re-opened. Anaesthesiologists blamed the problem on the inexperience of prison officials, stating that had correct execution procedures been followed, the complications would never have occurred. This error apparently led to Illinois' subsequent adoption of an alternative method of lethal injection.

At 12.17am on May 10, 1994, Gacy's heart stopped beating. Death was confirmed at 12.58am. 'He got a much easier death than any of his victims,' said prosecutor William Kunkle. Gacy's body was cremated after the execution, but not before his brain was removed. It became the possession of Helen Morrison, a trial defence witness, who interviewed Gacy and other serial killers in an attempt to isolate common personality traits of violent sociopaths. The Killer Clown's final statement to his lawyer before his execution was that killing him would not compensate for the loss of others, and that the state was murdering him. His final spoken words were: 'Kiss my ass.'

During his time at Menard Correctional Centre, Gacy took up studying visual arts, painting Disney characters, Michelangelo's 'Pieta' and self-portraits as Pogo The Clown. After his execution, the paintings became collectors' items. Many have been displayed at exhibitions and others have been sold at various auctions, with individual prices ranging between $200 and $20,000. Although Gacy was permitted to earn money from the sale of his paintings until 1985, he claimed his artwork was intended 'to bring joy into people's lives'. Some of the paintings were bought to be destroyed and in June 1994, a communal bonfire was held in Naperville, Illinois, attended by about 300 people, including relatives of nine of Gacy's victims. In 2017, Mullock's Auctions in Shropshire, England, auctioned off a number of his works, as well as crime scene pictures from the trial. Three of his paintings, including two originals entitled 'I'm Pogo The Clown' and 'They Call Him Mr. Gacy' sold for £4,000 and £325 respectively. Eight other works went unsold.

In October 2011, the Cook County Sheriff's office set out to finally put names to eight victims who remained unidentified. 'There is no time limit when we stop caring,' said Sheriff Thomas Dart. At a media conference he said investigators were actively seeking DNA samples from individuals across the U.S. related to any male missing between 1970 and 1979. Initially inundated with leads from hundreds of emails and telephone calls, over the ensuing seven years, detective Jason Moran managed to identify two of the victims. The work continues.

CHAPTER 4

ROBERT EDWARD CRANE

'I don't smoke, I don't drink. Two out of three ain't bad.'—Robert Crane.

COLONEL WILHELM KLINK. General Burkhalter. Oscar Schnitzer. Sergeant Hans Schultz. Corporal Louis LeBeau. The names may look familiar. Cast your mind back to the 1960s when television ran one of the funniest American sitcoms ever made about a fictional German Prisoner of War camp. Hogan's Heroes was centred on Stalag 13. Behind the fencing was a bunch of U.S. resistance fighters overseen by the strict but bumbling Colonel Klink, portrayed by Werner Klemperer. While the prisoners had an abnormal number of perks, that did not stop them from messing with their guards at every given opportunity as they fought the Allied war effort from within Germany. It was, after all, a television series made to entertain, and was not a visual history lesson.

The show was created by Bernard Fein and Albert S. Ruddy, and first aired on September 17, 1965. It ran for six seasons over 168 episodes, and its last hurrah was on April 4, 1971. It was not a grand finale. When CBS aired the episode entitled Rockets or Romance, it was deemed so unexceptional that Brenda Scott Royce's book Hogan's Heroes: Behind The Scenes At Stalag 13!, estimated its basic plot had been used eleven times before. Additionally, Donald Bevan and Edmund Trzcinski, the writers of the 1951 Broadway play *Stalag 17*, had filed a lawsuit against the creators of the series for plagiarism. The pair had drawn on their personal experiences as prisoners of a stalag in Austria during the war. Paramount Pictures turned their play into a 1953 feature film, directed by Billy Wilder and starring William Holden in an Academy Award-winning performance. The film was set in a German Prisoner of War camp and tracked the daily boredom and daring night-time escape attempts of the resident U.S. airmen. Bevan and Trzcinski unsuccessfully sued Bing Crosby Productions, Stalag 13's producer, for infringement. While the jury found in favour of the plaintiffs, the federal judge overruled them, finding a 'striking difference in the dramatic mood of the two works.' Aside from the lawsuit and the rather tardy end to the show, Hogan's Heroes won two Emmy awards out of 12 nominations. Both wins were for Werner Klemperer as Outstanding Supporting Actor, in 1968 and 1969. Klemperer also received nominations in the same category in 1966, 1967 and 1970. The series' other nominations were for Nita Talbot for Supporting Actress In A Comedy in 1968, Gordon Avil for Cinematography in 1968 and Bob Crane for Actor In A Comedy Series in 1966 and 1967.

Robert Edward Crane starred as Colonel Hogan. On June 28, 1978, seven years after the last episode aired, the actor drew his last breath—bludgeoned to death in his Scottsdale apartment. He was 49 years old.

Waterbury in Connecticut sits in leafy New England, and although its name may suggest this city of a little over 100,000 inhabitants is closely associated with water, it is most known for something else entirely. Also referred to as the Brass City, Waterbury is known for brass production and, as a natural result, as a large producer of clocks, watches and other timepieces. This is also a place of historical features, including lovingly preserved buildings. Crane was born here on July 13, 1928, to Alfred Thomas and Rosemary Crane, who already had one son, Alfred John. Of Irish and Russian descent, Crane was raised in a traditional Roman Catholic household. When he was about two years old, the family relocated to Stamford, Connecticut, where he and his brother grew up. In the mid-1930s Alfred Senior found work at a department store in Poughkeepsie, New York, before relocating the family back to Stamford in 1936.

From an early age, music played a large part in young Robert's life. He was heavily influenced by the American jazz drummer Eugene Bertram Krupa, whom he heard play at the New York World's Fair in April 1939. From that moment on, Crane wanted to be a drummer. Krupa was renowned for his energetic style and showmanship, appearing not only on stage but also in Hollywood films. Such was his reputation that Rolling Stone magazine put him at number seven in its list of the 100 greatest drummers of all time. By the time he was in middle school, Crane was drumming with the kids in his neighbourhood, forming bands and teaching his friends the rudiments of the drum kit to enable them to go on to play in local parades. He wasn't idle himself in that respect, playing in the school orchestra and marching band. Wherever Bob Crane went, the drumsticks went with him. In junior high school he and a bunch of neighborhood kids formed a jazz outfit called the Catino Band. Come high school and the band was growing in popularity, and a staple at school assemblies. By the time Crane was in his senior year, it had been renamed the Crane-Catino Band, gigging throughout Stamford, Greenich, Norwalk, Darien and other Connecticut communities. While still in high school, Crane also performed timpani with the Connecticut Symphony Orchestra (since renamed the Bridgeport Symphony Orchestra), as part of the orchestra's school music programme. School friends also recall him playing with the Norwalk Symphony Orchestra. One can imagine how these live performances enriched Crane's life. He was a happy, good-natured teenager, his school friends recalling him being somewhat reserved yet always ready to make them laugh. That sunny personality presented him as a caring individual with a sensitive side, ever conscious of not wanting to hurt anyone's feelings.

Crane graduated from Stamford High School in 1946, at which time he took employment at Finlay Straus jewellery store as a watch repairman and salesman. The store was located on the right side of Main Street, a section that no longer exists. Stamford at the time was a bustling town where everyone knew everybody else. In 1948 Crane began service in the Connecticut Army National Guard and was honourably discharged after two years. He began sending audition tapes to radio stations along America's East Coast. As rejections came back, he was far from discouraged, instead taking a course at the University of Bridgeport in station operation, under the instruction of radio personality Wally Dunlap, of WICC. On May 20, 1949, Crane married his high school sweetheart Anne Terzian, after dating for two years. The couple had three children, Robert David, Deborah Anne and Karen Leslie. Crane got his big break in 1950 when he received a call out of the blue from WLEA in Hornell, New York, offering him his first job in radio. The station broadcast a talk radio format. He quickly settled into the role, achieving the position of programme director before he left in December 1950, having decided to take up an offer at WBIS, a radio station licensed to serve Bristol, Connecticut. Once again, he quickly made his mark and was promoted to senior announcer and programme director. It was to prove a short tenure, for come April 1951, hardly five months into the role, he went to WLIZ in Bridgeport, Connecticut, and back on home territory—just where he wanted to be. It was a somewhat bizarre situation. Wally Dunlap, whose college course Crane had attended, was looking for a new morning man who did not drink alcohol. Crane didn't and so was offered the slot.

WLIZ purchased WICC for $190,000 on November 17, 1951, and Crane's show moved to the new station. It was not long before he was promoted to programme director. He also worked at WICC's UHF television station, Channel 43, with well-known Bridgeport figure Morgan Kaolian. Despite their best efforts, the station, in its infancy, floundered. Crane gave his final morning show in WICC on August 11, 1956, before moving his family to Los Angeles. On September 3 he launched his radio show to Southern California audiences, joining CBS Radio and hosting a morning show at KNX. He proved an instant hit with listeners, topping the morning ratings thanks in no small part to his humour and drumming skills, and becoming a skilled interviewer. He could not resist the temptation to play the drums along to the tunes he was playing. Between September 13, 1956, and August 16, 1965, he interviewed more than 3,000 people, including Bob Hope, Jerry Lewis, Richard Chamberlain and Bette Davis.

'The first station I started out with was a 250-watt station,' said Crane in an interview. 'I went to a 1,000-watt station, which was the Bridgeport station. And from the 1,000-watt, I went to the 50,000-watt, which is quite a jump, and it has happened to a lot of people. It's a fortunate thing to be in the right place at the right time.' It was probably only natural that with his bubbly radio personality, his excellent celebrity-biased interview technique and the popularity of his radio show that the offers started rolling in from producers to host his own television talk show. However, not wanting to transfer his radio show to television, he turned down all offers, although he guest-hosted and filled in for Jack Parr on The Tonight Show and for Johnny Carson on Who Do You Trust? No, Bob Crane had his sights set on something else entirely—acting.

By 1959 he was performing in community theatre. Two years later, when a no-acting clause expired with KNX, he began picking up bit parts in television and film. Ironically, one of his earliest television roles was as a radio announcer on The Twilight Zone, when he was heard but not seen. In 1962 he appeared in The Dick Van Dyke Show as Harry Rogers in the episode called Somebody Has To Play Cleopatra. People took notice of his acting talents, including Donna Reed, and he landed a permanent role on The Donna Reed Show as Dr David Kelsey. His was a hectic schedule, working at KNX and on the show from 1963 to 1965, but it was when Crane began to take his role as an actor seriously.

In 1964 he enrolled for a course under the direction of Stella Adler, whose method of teaching emphasised that authenticity in acting was achieved by drawing on inner reality to expose deep emotional experience. Believing that theatre existed 99 per cent in the imagination, she drew on

Konstantin Stanislavski's System that the source of acting was imagination and key to its problems was truth: truth in the circumstances of the play. A wealthy Russian businessman turned director, Stanislavski founded the Moscow Art Theatre and his system of acting was spread throughout the world by his students. To bring forth the real meaning in a character, an actor needed both imagination and the ability to open oneself up emotionally. One of the greatest exponents of this art was the great Marlon Brando, who enrolled in Erwin Piscator's Dramatic Workshop at New York's New School and came into Stella Adler's orbit. The results of this meeting between actor and teacher marked a watershed in American acting and culture, as it was through Brando that 'The Method' was introduced into American theatre and film. Stella was a major inspiration to her students. Her mantra was: 'You act with your soul. That's why you all want to be actors—because your souls are not used up by life.'

It had been through the encouragement of Donna Reed that Crane took the course, and he went on to improve his technique and grow as an actor, which in turn made him restless for something different to the role he had on her show. On December 1, 1964, he was released from The Donna Reed Show. That, in turn, prompted a flood of offers from producers for him to star in various television series, including Please Don't Eat The Daisies, and My Mother The Car. He turned them all down, except for one. In December 1964, Crane was approached about the production of a new show set during the Second World War. Having read the script, he spoke with producer Edward H. Feldman and decided to audition. Three days before Christmas, he had a screen test with Werner Klemperer. The chemistry between the two actors was nothing short of instant, and Crane was offered the part of Colonel Robert E Hogan in the new comedy series Hogan's Heroes. Having agreed to film the pilot episode in January 1965, Crane was acutely conscious of not causing offence to war veterans and former PoWs. A trailer without a soundtrack or laughter track was sent to groups of veterans in the Midwest, seeking their thoughts. They loved it, stating that without humour, they would never have made it through the war. Set in Stalag 13, the sit-com involved the sabotage and espionage missions of Allied soldiers, led by Hogan, from under the noses of the Germans. It was a hit from the first episode. There was no way Crane could pass up the opportunity to play the distinctive military-style snare drum rhythm that introduced the show's theme song. There were detractors to the sit-com theme, believing that it would make fun of the Holocaust and concentration camps. They had missed the point, because while the finger of fun would be pointed at the Germans, it would never swing towards either the war or its serious implications. 'I think we make great fools of the Germans,' Robert Clary, who played spirited Corporal Louis LeBeau, said in a 1966 interview, 'we are laughing at them.' In another interview later, Crane concurred: 'I've had people ask me, how can you make fun of a concentration camp? Think of all the Jews who were killed. Well, ours isn't a concentration camp; it's a camp filled with soldiers who are prisoners. And their situations can be funny.'

In August 1965, Crane resigned from KNX to concentrate all his efforts on his acting career. While the hit series was playing out, however, Crane's marriage was in freefall. By 1968 he had begun an affair with Patricia Annette Olson, who played Fräulein Hilda under the stage name Sigrid Valdis. Hilda was bumbling Colonel Klink's second secretary for seasons two to six. Despite her German blood, she would aid Hogan and his men in exchange for candy, stockings and kisses from Hogan—kisses that were also played out in private. In 1970, Crane divorced his wife just prior to their 21st anniversary, and later the same year married Patricia on the set of the show. His best man was Richard Dawson, who played Corporal Peter Newkirk. Bob and Patricia's son, Robert Scott, was born in 1971, and they adopted their teenage housekeeper, Ana Marie. The Cranes separated in December 1977. As Crane happily settling into his second marriage, the new president of CBS abruptly cancelled Hogan's Heroes after a six-year run that had lasted longer than America's involvement in the war. It was nothing short of an unceremonious dumping. Even when the sit-com M.A.S.H. ended a year later, it had enjoyed a two-and-a-half-hour finale and watched by a record-breaking audience, eager to see how the men and women of the 4077th handled the end of the Korean War. Hogan's Heroes simply ended; there was no successful escape for the men, with the gates of Luftwaffe Stalag 13 thrown open for their walk to freedom, no fanfare—nothing.

April 4, 1971, proved to be a dark day for Hogan's Heroes in more ways than one. By season six, while still carrying some sense of humour, the show had taken on more serious undertones than what had originally been produced in series one. In the final episode, the prisoners got word that the Germans were deploying a new secret weapon to help them win the war. The men set out to distract camp Kommandant Colonel Klink and his wingman Sergeant Schultz until the weapons could be disarmed. The episode went out with hardly a fizzle before the series expired for good. CBS was in the process of bringing more sophisticated fare to the viewing public, and the sit-com was part of the cupboard clear-out. In all probability, the morphing of sit-com to drama with dry humour had proved to be its nemesis.

Undeterred, Crane pursued his acting career, picking up roles which, for the most part, proved unfulfilling. He appeared in two Disney films, Superdad in 1973, and Guss in 1976, and in between had guest spots on shows including Police Woman and Ellery Queen. In 1977 he appeared in The Love Boat. In Superdad he played Charlie McCready, and the plot revolved around him attempting to wrest his daughter Wendy, played by Kathleen Cody, from her child-hood friends, as he believed they had no ambition. The one person he especially disapproved of was her boyfriend Bart, played by Kurt Russell. In one scene, to bridge the generation gap, McCready falls off a surfboard and gets washed up—a bit like the film, which sat on the shelf for a year before flopping at the box office.

In 1975, Crane was given his own show, but NBC pulled it after only three months. The comedy revolved around the character Bob Wilcox, who decided to leave his insurance job to enter medical school and needing the support of his family to deal with the curriculum and being older. Produced by MTM Enterprises, the series was filmed with a three-camera set up in front of a studio audience, with a sweetened laughter track. At the outset Crane had expressed his desire that the series should be what he called 'hard comedy', which he described as comedy that 'goes for the fences. It's also what you might call take-a-risk comedy because if you don't hit a home run, you might strike out. It's either a belly-laugh or it's no go and no show.' As it transpired, it was a flop.

Crane had maintained a keen interest in the theatre since his time in Connecticut, performing in numerous productions from the 1950s to the 1970s. He first toured in 1969 in the play Cactus Flower, which was so well received that he hoped to use it as a springboard to Broadway. In 1973, Crane had bought the rights to the play Beginner's Luck, in which he both directed and starred. The play travelled the country, showing in California, Texas and Hawaii. In June 1978, he took it to Scottsdale, Arizona. Back then, the building at the southeast corner of Scottsdale Road and Shea Boulevard was known as the Windmill Dinner Theatre. It was here that Crane was performing with 28-year-old Australian-born actress Victoria Berry. They had been touring for months. Berry had been failing to fulfill her ambition for the Hollywood spotlight. She had auditioned for Charlie's Angels after Farrah Fawcett-Majors quit the show, but Cheryl Ladd lucked out on that one. She had also been set to play the part of Marilyn Monroe in a film to be called Saint Marilyn, but that deal fell through. Some may remember her as the go-go dancer in the credits of Starsky and Hutch. So here she was instead, on stage with Crane on the dinner theatre circuit, paying the bills and working on her acting skills. She'd met Crane years earlier when her future husband Alan Wells had introduced them. Wells at one time had owned a Los Angeles Strip Club called the Classic Cat, a dive much favoured by Crane.

On the evening of June 26, 1978, it was business as usual at the Windmill. Berry was seated for a while in the audience alongside John Carpenter, Crane's best friend who hailed from California. After the curtain fell for the evening, Berry saw the two men walking towards Crane's car. The following afternoon, at about 2pm, Berry turned up at the Winfield Apartments, 7430 East Chaparral in Scottsdale, to meet Crane. She later volunteered to detectives that she had twice slept with her fellow actor. On this occasion, she said, it was not for sex but to dub a new voice track over a scene from the play. Arriving at Apartment 132-A, Berry knocked on the door. There was no answer. As the door happened to be unlocked, she stepped inside and called out Crane's name. There was no reply, and the place was in darkness. She pulled back a curtain and looked out at the swimming pool, but Crane wasn't there. She then went into the bedroom. In interviews with police, Berry described what she saw in the bed.

'At first, I thought it was a girl with long, dark hair, because all the blood had turned real dark. I thought oh, Bob's got a girl here. Now, where's Bob? I thought well, she's done something to herself. Bob has gone to get help. At that time, I recognised blood… it was like a strange feeling.' As she approached the lifeless body, curled up in a fetal position, she realised it was, in fact, Bob Crane, and noticed an electric cord was tied around his neck in a bow.

The first Scottsdale officer to arrive on scene was Paulette Kasieta, who later would work as an investigator for the Public Defender's Office and work on behalf of defendant John Carpenter in the subsequent murder investigation and trial. Police Lieutenant Ron Dean took over the scene mid-afternoon. As Berry was writing her statement in the kitchen, the apartment phone jangled. Dean told her to answer it and not to mention the unfolding event. At the end of the line was John Carpenter, who explained that he was back in Los Angeles. Dean then took the receiver and told Carpenter he was investigating 'an incident at the Crane apartment'. Carpenter told the officer he had been with Crane until about 1am, which he later revised to 2.45am, before making his way to the airport. The next caller was a female friend of the actor, and the call after that was from Bob Crane Jr., worried about his father after he had received a telephone call from Carpenter, who himself called a second time.

In January 1978, filming had begun for a pilot episode for a proposed new television series entitled The Hawaiian Experience. Hosted by Crane, the idea was for him to provide viewers with a behind-the-scenes look at various resorts, people and cultures on the Hawaiian Islands. The shoot ran into problems from the start and never made it into homes due to the brutal murder of its irreverent host. That same month, Crane had also filmed an episode of the Canadian television series Celebrity Cooks. It aired on several occasions in Canada before it was snapped up to run in U.S. syndication. A CBS affiliate network executive then pulled the episode from the line-up because it had been scheduled to air only days after Crane's murder.

Word of the actor's demise spread like wildfire across the valley and onwards to the outside world. Scottsdale suddenly had become global news. The police department certainly wasn't ready for what unfolded; it didn't even have a murder unit, because murder hardly ever happened in Scottsdale. Chief case officer Dennis Borkenhagen and his superior, Lieutenant Ron Dean, led the investigation and began with a sweep of the crime scene. How and why the killer had struck were primary concerns for the team. Nothing of financial value was missing from the apartment, so that eliminated robbery. There was no evidence of a struggle. A post-mortem examination later revealed that Crane had been asleep when he had been bludgeoned to death in the left temple with a blunt instrument. The murder weapon was missing. There were bloodstains on the inside of the front door but no signs of forced entry. It was, essentially, a complete mystery.

When the investigators came to interview Crane's friends, colleagues and acquaintances, despite him being amiable, they were surprised to note how many detested him. There was his estranged second wife, a fellow actor, husbands and boyfriends of women Crane bedded. Some of those females had posed naked for the actor and his Polaroid camera. Detectives came across videotapes and a mini darkroom complete with negatives of nude women awaiting development. While the investigation opened the door on Crane's alternate sex-driven lifestyle, shortly before his death he had seen a counsellor to whom he admitted being a sex addict and was looking to be healed. His counsellor described him as a 'tremendous talent' and someone who 'just happened to be famous', and who had 'weaknesses and foibles like the rest of us'. While the tapes and photographs proved a matter of fascination for the investigators, their attention was focused on Crane's friend John Carpenter, then a regional sales manager for Sony Electronics. He had helped Crane with his video hobby.

Unable to produce hard evidence or even clarify a motive, investigators thought they were onto something on June 30 after Carpenter returned to Los Angeles, when they located the 1978 Chrysler Cordoba he'd rented for part of his four-day stay in Phoenix. Carpenter had complained of a faulty electrical system and Avis had sent the vehicle to Lanker Chrysler-Plymouth, a Phoenix dealership, for repairs. There detective Darwin Barrie saw what appeared to be dried blood on the car's interior passenger side. Having contacted his supervisor, Lieutenant Ron Dean, the vehicle was taken to the state Department of Public Safety compound in Phoenix for scientific examination. The blood group, type B, matched that of Crane, which was only found in about one out of seven people, but the DPS was unable to prove that the blood actually came from Crane. Carpenter had no explanation for the blood's presence.

Upon being told he was the number one suspect, Carpenter voluntarily returned to Arizona for further questioning on July 2 in the company of detectives Dean and Borkenhagen. He declined to have an attorney present and was happy to take a lie detector test—anything, in fact, to prove his innocence. At the time of the murder, Carpenter was separated from his wife Diana, and was living with 20-year-old Rita Cloutier in Inglewood, California. He didn't know it, but he was on a one-way ticket to Arizona. At Scottsdale Police Department, Carpenter was interviewed in the presence of Dean, Borkenhagen and deputy county attorney Larry Turoff. With no other evidence, the Maricopa County Attorney declined to file charges.

Twenty-two years later in 1990, the case was re-opened when Scottsdale Police Detective Barry Vassall and Maricopa County Attorney's Office Investigator Jim Raines, a former Phoenix homicide investigator, re-examined the evidence from 1978. Raines had discovered a photograph of the car's interior that appeared to show a piece of brain tissue.

Although the actual tissue samples originally recovered from the car had been lost, an Arizona judge ruled that the new evidence was admissible. In June 1992, John Carpenter was arrested and charged with the murder. During the trial in 1994, Robert Crane Jr. testified that in the weeks leading up to his father's death, Crane had repeatedly expressed a desire to sever his friendship with Carpenter, telling his son that Carpenter had become 'a hanger-on' and 'a nuisance to the point of being obnoxious'. 'My dad expressed that he just didn't need Carpenter kind of hanging around him anymore,' he told the court. Also, he testified that Crane had called Carpenter the night before the murder and ended their friendship.

The prosecution's case was attacked by Carpenter's attorneys as being circumstantial and inconclusive. The murder weapon had never been identified or found, and the prosecution's theory that a camera tripod had been used in the attack was speculation based solely on Carpenter's occupation. They disputed the claim that the newly discovered evidence photo showed brain tissue and presented many examples of 'sloppy work' by the police, such as the mishandling and misplacing of evidence—including the crucial tissue sample. They then presented evidence which included witnesses from the restaurant where the two men had dined the evening prior to the murder, showing that Carpenter and Crane had still been the best of friends. Carpenter was acquitted and continued to maintain his innocence until his death four years later, in 1998.

Robert Crane Jr., however, continued to speculate publicly, suggesting that his father's widow, Patricia Olson, might have had a role in instigating the crime. He alluded to Crane's will, which excluded him, his siblings and his mother, and left the entire estate to Patricia. Crane Jr. was happy to repeat his suspicions in a 2015 book called Crane: Sex, Celebrity, and My Father's Unsolved Murder. In November 2016, Phoenix television reporter John Hook received permission from the Maricopa County Attorney's Office to submit the 1978 blood samples from Carpenter's rental car for re-testing. The reasoning was to use a more advanced DNA technique than the one that had been adopted in 1990. Two sequences were identified, one from an unknown male, and the other too degraded to reach a conclusion. This round of testing consumed the entire remaining DNA from the rental car, making further tests impossible.

Bob Crane's took place on July 5, 1978, at St Paul the Apostle Catholic Church in Westwood. It was attended by an estimated 200 family members and friends. The pallbearers included Hogan's Heroes producer Edward Feldman, co-stars Larry Hovis and Robert Clary, and Robert Jr. Crane was buried at Oakwood Memorial Park in Chatsworth, Los Angeles County. In 2003, Patricia Olson had his remains relocated to the prestigious Westwood Memorial Park on Glendon Avenue in Los Angeles. Located in the middle of the memorial park, his elaborate marker contains writings and photographs of him and his widow, who was buried under her stage name of Sigrid Valdis after she died from lung cancer in 2007.

In the end, radio personality Bob Crane only ever had one hit television show plus a few guest spots, minor roles in a couple of Disney films, and a failed TV pilot before his downward spiral led him to the dinner theatre circuit, which is how he came to be treading the boards in Scottsdale on that fateful night in June 1978. Hogan's Heroes may have timeless appeal due to its Second World War setting. It will never really age but then, Bob Crane will never get past 49.

On Sunday, October 2, 2011, 57 of Crane's high school friends and classmates from the class of 1946 gathered at the Italian Centre in Stamford for Stamford High School's 65th class reunion. It was a time to catch up, have fun and reminisce. The class of '46 had been large, with 537 seniors graduating on June 5, Bob Crane among them. The close-knit group had grown up during the Great Depression and were the first class from Stamford to graduate after the Second World War. In June 1976, Crane attended his 30th class reunion—the last time he and his school friends saw each other. Two years later one of the first disc jockeys in the country to earn in excess of $100,000 a year was dead.

Down on his luck and pretty much down on finances in the mid to late 1970s, shortly after Crane's murder, his estate came into millions of dollars from a new syndication deal for Hogan's Heroes, which he owned a small part of. He once said: 'Eventually, what you're looking for is gonna happen, and by the time it does happen, you'll be that much better along the way to what you should be. Don't get discouraged, and just keep on plugging along, and what you want will eventually be yours. You know, there's nothing to stop it if you just keep on working hard. And by working hard, I mean doing the best job you possibly can. Everything happens for the best, and I believe it completely.'

Crane had found fame in the age of the leading man and those all-American heroes, alongside the likes of Robert Culp and Robert Conrad. There are, however, some ironies at work here. The play Beginner's Luck was about a man having an extramarital affair. Crane was going through a bitter divorce at the time of his murder. Because it wasn't final, his wife inherited his estate; a fact that so rankled his son. One of the last episodes of Hogan's Heroes was entitled Hogan's Double Life. The actor's once secret Jekyll-and-Hyde lifestyle shocked his fans when it was exposed and went viral, and it still resonates today. We can put that one down to the nature of fame and the double-edged sword of celebrity status, where we love our heroes on the ascendancy and also love to read about them as they spiral downwards, often with their reputation in tatters. Much of it is about breaking through the façade. Is the person we watch on screen really who we think they are? In the case of Bob Crane, we know there was a dark side. In his book, Robert Crane Jr. described him as 'the Pied Piper of Porn', writing that his father was obsessed with both watching pornography and making his own, as well as having a voracious sexual appetite. It is perhaps a sad fact of life that the public tends to dwell on that dark, private side of his life. Crane has been the subject of several books and numerous documentaries. His case also remains popular on true crime podcasts. The full-length biographical film, Auto Focus, starred Greg Kinnear as Bob Crane, in which the film Superdad was featured. In it, Crane was portrayed in the role as the leading man in the Disney film as a way to revive his career after Hogan's Heroes had been retired. It glimpsed into his colourful life and mysterious death. No doubt Crane capitalised on his fame, indulging in numerous affairs and delving into the seedier side of sex and strip clubs. Even though it is now decades old, Hogan's Heroes continues as a timeless capsule in our lives, as does the actor who portrayed the hero, a man who was in reality working 15-hour days locked up in Stalag 13 in Culver City, portraying the affable Colonel Hogan five days a week. As his salacious private life imploded after his untimely and grisly end, it extinguished the red-light that had forever been on in his makeshift film processing lab.

Patricia Olson and her son Scotty managed to burn through Crane's two jumbo life insurance policies of $400,000 each, plus proceeds from the sale of the house she and Crane had lived in, which was worth a million dollars. And don't let's forget the yearly receipts from the Hogan's Heroes residuals. When Robert Jr. learned of Olson's death, he auctioned off his father's leather jacket and shirt from his costume on Hogan's Heroes. It sold for $32,000. While he may have put his father's memory to rest, the case remains open.

CHAPTER 5

KENNETH BIANCHI AND ANGELO BUONO JR.

THE HILLSIDE STRANGLERS

'I'm not saying nothing is wrong with me, sir. I'm not saying that at all. I don't believe I am perfectly well. But what is well? I'm not a psychologist.'—Kenneth Bianchi.

IT CAN be great fun, searching for buried treasure. People will discard the most extraordinary things. Head to the local tip and car boots will be spilling over with bin bags full of goodness knows what. Household items, garden refuse, garage clear-outs and old mattresses. That's what a nine-year-old boy was scrambling over in order to get a better look at a couple of mannequins that had been junked with the rest of the trash. Only they weren't mannequins, they were human bodies: two small girls, aged

12 and 14, stripped naked and left to rot in the sun with the rest of the detritus, attracted by a small, inquisitive boy and swarms of insects.

The date was February 16, 1978. Dolly Cepeda and Sonja Johnson had been missing for a week. The girls were not the only ones to turn up dead. For four months the hills around Los Angeles had been littered with the bodies of young women and girls—the work of the Hillside Strangler. Terror had been present in the city since October 16, 1977; four months of never knowing when the killer would strike next. As night fell on the discovery of the two young girls, there would be another murder for Los Angeles to contend with. In the space of 30 days, five girls were dumped in the hills, having been raped, tortured and murdered. Five children from the age of 12 but less than half the number of victims of the Hillside Strangler. Make that stranglers, because this was the work of cousins Kenneth 'Kenny' Alessio Bianchi and Angelo Buono Jr. Another two victims would be attributed to Bianchi alone. It would be almost a year before he was apprehended, followed by Buono nine months later.

Angelo Buono was born on October 5, 1934, in Rochester, New York. His parents, Italian immigrants, divorced when he was young. Having gained custody of her five-year-old son, his mother Jenny moved across the country with young Angelo and her daughter Cecilia to live in Glendale, California. By the age of 14, Buono was stealing cars and started calling his mother by demeaning names, such as 'whore'. He had become fascinated with the sex offender Caryl

Chessman, dubbed the Red-Light Rapist. He considered him as his hero, even though he was said to have thought that Chessman should have killed his victims as well as sexually assaulting them. In 1950, aged 16, he dropped out of school and was arrested for larceny. Sent to reform school for grand theft auto, he managed to escape, only to be recaptured by the California Youth Authority.

In 1955 Buono married his childhood sweetheart, 17-year-old Geraldine Vinal, but left her less than a week later. Geraldine, carrying Buono's child, gave birth to Michael Lee Buono on January 10, 1956. Having divorced, Buono refused to pay child maintenance or to allow his son to call him 'Father'. In late 1956, Buono's second son, Angelo Anthony Buono III, was born to Mary Catherine Castillo. The couple married on April 5, 1957 and went on to have four more children: Peter in 1957, Danny in 1958, Louis in 1960 and Grace, born two years later. In the same year, Buono was jailed for petty theft. His wife filed for divorce in 1964 on the grounds of her husband's perverse sexual desires and violence. She had tried for reconciliation but when Buono handcuffed her and threatened to kill her after shoving a gun into her stomach, unsurprisingly she'd had enough. Buono then moved in with Nanette Campina, a 25-year-old single mother of two, and treated her in the same way. Campina was desperate to leave him but feared that he'd kill her if she did, so continued in the relationship. In 1967, aged 33, Buono was sentenced to a year in prison for car theft but because of his large family and the need for him to work, the sentence was suspended. In the same year, his girlfriend gave birth to Tony, their first child together and Buono's seventh. In 1969 their second child, Sam, was born. By 1971, Nanette had suffered enough of Buono's abuse: he had been bragging to his friends about raping her 14-year-old daughter. She took the children and left the state, getting as far away as possible. The following year, Buono married Deborah Taylor. The two never lived together and never bothered to divorce. By 1975, Buono had built himself a reasonable reputation as an auto upholsterer, working on his own in the back of his apartment at 703 East Colorado Street. He had also earned a reputation as a stud and enjoyed referring to himself as The Italian Stallion. One of the young girls attracted to him twice became pregnant. She aborted the first child and suffered a miscarriage during her second pregnancy.

Buono's cousin, Kenneth Alessio Bianchi, was born on May 22, 1951, also in Rochester. Bianchi's 17-year-old mother was a prostitute and an alcoholic. Unable to care for her son, he was put up for adoption and was taken in by local residents Nicholas Bianchi and Frances Sciolono. Despite a stable upbringing, he turned into a pathological liar and would spend much time daydreaming, which was attributed to petit mal seizures when he was five years old. He was also diagnosed with passive-aggressive personality disorder, which can affect a person's ability to create and maintain healthy relationships, with parenting style, family dynamics and other childhood influences acting as contributing factors. An intelligent child with an IQ of 116, he was an under-achiever at school. To change her son's ways, his mother sent him to a private Catholic elementary school. When Nicholas Bianchi died from pneumonia in 1964, unemotional Bianchi had to leave and attend a public high school, graduating in 1971. He married his high school sweetheart Brenda Beck, but that marriage lasted a mere eight months before the couple divorced.

Keen to join the police service, Bianchi enrolled at Monroe Community College, part of the State University of New York, to study police science and psychology but he dropped out after one term. This was followed by another setback when he was rejected for a position at the sheriff's department. What followed was a series of menial jobs before he landed a position as a security guard at a jewellery store. That didn't last long either, as he was fired for stealing and passing on his ill-gotten gains to his various girlfriends. Bianchi moved to Los Angeles in 1975, and in January the following year he met up with and then moved in with his older adoptive cousin, Angelo Buono. A chronic liar, he set up a psychology practice with a bogus degree. Still with a keen interest in working with the police, Bianchi applied for jobs at two local police departments but neither had any available positions. In July 1976 he secured a job at California Land Title Company and spent his first pay cheque on an apartment and a Cadillac. He moved in with his girlfriend Kelli Boyd, whom he had met at work and told he was dying of cancer. In May 1977, she announced she was pregnant with his child and Bianchi proposed. She refused but continued to stay with him.

It is believed that Angelo Buono acted as a role model for his younger cousin, and subsequently was able to sway him, teaching him how to use a fake police badge to extort free sex from prostitutes. In September 1977, Buono hit on the idea that they should become pimps, forcing teenage runaways no one would miss to turn tricks for them. They had limited success, as their first two girls, Sabra Hannan and Becky Spears, escaped—but not before suffering abuse at the hands of Buono. Spears happened upon a lawyer by the name of David Wood who, having learned of the girls' situation, helped them escape from the city. 'I was tired of getting beat up, tired of all the threats, and tired of engaging in prostitution,' Hannan later told a jury when the men who tortured her were put on trial for murder. Impersonating police officers, it wasn't long before the cousins came across a new girl. When the cousins tried to recruit more punters, things turned sour.

In October 1977 they were conned into buying a 'trick list' from a prostitute named Deborah Noble and her friend Yolanda Washington, which supposedly held the names of men who frequented prostitutes. Realising they had been ripped off and unable to find Noble, they went after Washington. On October 18, 1977, police discovered the naked body of the 19-year-old, single black mother, still with the fabric around her neck that had been used to strangle her. She had been casually laid out on open grass near the

Ventura Highway on the edge of Forest Lawn Memorial Park in Hollywood Hills, one of six Forest Lawn cemeteries in southern California. She had been bound, raped and strangled.

Washington was born on August 28, 1977, in Glendale, Los Angeles County. While she listed her occupation as a waitress at the International House of Pancakes, one of a long-standing chain serving a variety of pancakes and other American breakfast and dinner fare, she was, in fact, a street prostitute. She had been picked up by the cousins who had posed as plain clothes policemen, and subsequently murdered in their car before her body was left at 6510 Forest Lawn Drive. Called to the scene, Frank Salerno of the Los Angeles Sheriff's Department determined that the corpse had been cleaned before being dumped. Faint marks were visible around the neck, wrists and ankles where a rope had been used. Music store owner Ronald LeMieux was the last person to see her alive: he later testified that two men flashing police badges had pulled Washington off the street, handcuffed her and pushed her into the back seat of an unmarked car. That would become Bianchi and Buono's trademark for most of their murders.

It wasn't long before the pair struck again. Located adjacent to Angeles National Forest, La Crescenta-Montrose retains a distinct, suburban vibe. Nestled between the much larger San Fernando and San Gabriel valleys, it is possible to drive anywhere from Pasadena to downtown Los Angeles in 30 minutes. At the end of the Civil War, American veterans began to drift into the valley with its warm, dry air, the perfect place to convalesce. Sanatoriums began to spring up, Kimbal and Rockhaven becoming famous for their celebrity patients during Hollywood's early era and through its Golden Age. The resultant towns that sprang up around these places of healing brought in well-to-do families seeking country living, but still close to Los Angeles' urban amenities. It was here, on October 31, that the cousins raped, sodomised and strangled 15-year-old Judith Ann Miller, before posing her legs in a diamond shape. The former Hollywood High School student was a runaway and occasional sex worker. She was last seen alive talking to a man driving a large two-tone sedan next to Carnet's Diner in the 8300 Block of Sunset Boulevard, West Hollywood. Posing as undercover officers, unsuspecting Miller was handcuffed before being driven to Buono's upholstery shop at 703 W. Colorado Boulevard, Glendale, where she was murdered. Her body was dumped in a flood control channel across from 2844 Alta Terrace, in the middle-class residential area of La Crescenta. A homeowner had covered her body with a tarp so neighbourhood children would not see her on their way to school. Ligature marks were found on her neck, wrists and ankles. Frank Salerno was quickly on the scene and found a small piece of light-coloured fluff on the victim's eyelid, which he carefully saved for the forensic team.

Born on December 10, 1955, in Los Angeles County, 21-year-old Elissa Teresa 'Lissa' Kastin worked in West Hollywood as a dancer and waitress. She was an original member of the L.A. Knockers, an all-female cabaret dance troupe formed in 1974 and proved popular throughout the 1970s and 1980s. The troupe performed at The Starwood, The Troubadour, The Comedy Store, The Matrix Theater and the Playboy Club, and to packed houses in Las Vegas and Reno. The group's dance/magic was brought together by principal choreographer Jennifer Stace, assisted by Marilyn Corwin, who worked her disco moves with The Village People. The troupe also caught the eye of Frank Zappa who, on New Year's Eve 1976, played a show at The Forum in Los Angeles with troupe members dressed as babies in diapers and white Afro wigs. Kastin became the cousins' third victim on November 5, 1977. As she drove home from work, the killers followed her and pulled over her car. Presenting a fake police badge, they said they were detectives and handcuffed her, saying she needed to be taken in for questioning. She was beaten, raped and strangled, and her body was left on a highway embankment near the Chevy Chase Country Club in Glendale. Author Darcy O'Brien noted in 1985's The Hillside Stranglers that Kastin was not 'an attractive enough victim' for the degenerate cousins who were put off by her 'health nut looks' and 'unshaved legs.' She was referred to as 'the ugly girl' among the killers' female body count, due to a photograph used by the newspapers and which, by all accounts, was not a true reflection of the young rising star of the stage.

Four days later, the nearly nude body of Jill Barcomb was discovered on a dirt path south of Mulholland Drive at

Franklin Canyon Drive, in West Los Angeles. The 18-year-old had been raped and strangled with a pair of blue trousers—but not at the hands of Buono and Bianchi, although they were originally the key suspects. She was found in a knee-to-chest position, naked from the waist down. According to Los Angeles County Coroner's Office, she had three bite marks on her right breast. Barcomb had been in southern California less than three weeks, having relocated from Oneida, New York, after a conviction for prostitution. The Barcomb investigation had been part of the Hillside Strangler Task Force, but when chief suspects Angelo Buono and Kenneth Bianchi were later eliminated, the investigation hit a dead end for two decades. That was until 2005, when cold case LAPD detectives Jose Ramirez and Cliff Shepard retrieved vital biological evidence, preserved over the years, and submitted it for DNA testing. Once uploaded to the California Offender DNA Index System database, the comparison returned with a hit. 'Jill Barcomb was killed by a cold-blooded person who violated and demeaned her,' LAPD spokesman Lieutenant Paul Vernon said, in 2005. 'Thankfully, through science and persistence we can say a dangerous serial predator has been identified.' That person was Rodney Alcala, a convicted sex offender who was at the time in Orange County Jail awaiting a third re-trial for the murder of a 12-year-old girl in 1979. A grand jury indictment in this case and two more murders in 1977 and 1978 was announced against Alcala, then aged 62. He was convicted on all counts and imprisoned for life.

On November 17, 1977, 17-year-old high school student Kathleen Robinson became the cousins' next victim. Robinson had been living with her mother and was a frequent hitchhiker. She had last been seen alive near the beach in Santa Monica. There were some unusual facts here, compared to the other Buono-Bianchi killings: when her body was found, she was fully clothed, and she was discovered in the flatland business section near Pico Boulevard of the city's post Wiltshire district, while other victims were discovered on hillsides in parks or residential areas. It was during this month that Catharine Lorre Baker, the 24-year-old daughter of the Hungarian born American character actor Peter Lorre, famous for his roles in such films as The Maltese Falcon, had a lucky escape. Having approached her, presumably with the intention of abducting her, Bianchi and Buono were looking through her identification papers when they found a photo of her sitting on her father's lap. Once they realised who her father was, they let her go. It was only after the cousins were arrested that Catharine realised they were the same men.

On November 20, a small boy discovered the bodies of 14-year-old Sonja Johnson and 12-year-old Dolores 'Dolly' Cepeda in Elysian Park. The girls had been raped and strangled. Johnson, whose family home was at Eagle Rock, had been a student at St Ignatius School in Highland Park and had been missing for a week. She had last been seen at Eagle Rock Plaza with Dolly, who attended the same school. The girls boarded an RTD bus in front of The Eagle Rock Plaza, homeward bound. The last time they were seen was when they alighted from a bus on York Boulevard and Avenue 46 and approached the passenger side of a large two-tone sedan, which reportedly had two men inside. The girls' bodies had already begun to decompose when they were found by the nine-year-old boy hunting for treasure on a trash heap near Dodger Stadium, in the Elysian Park neighbourhood of Los Angeles.

Later that same day, hikers stumbled upon the naked body of 20-year-old Kristina Weckler, who lived in an apartment at 809 E. Garfield Avenue in Glendale, on a hillside between Glendale and Eagle Rock. The honours student had attended the Pasadena Art Center College of Design, described by LAPD detective Bob Grogan as a 'loving and serious young woman who should have had a bright future ahead of her.' Ligature marks were found on her wrists, ankles and neck, and there were also bruises to her breast and two puncture marks on her arm. This time the killer had brutalised and strangled his victim, and had also injected her with Windex, a glass and hard-surface cleaning fluid: a clear case of sadistic refinement. Bianchi lived in the same apartment complex as Weckler and when police interviewed him, he was not considered as a suspect. Three days later, the badly decomposed body of 28-year-old scientologist and aspiring actress Jane Evelyn King was found dumped at the southbound Los Feliz off-ramp of the Golden Gate Freeway. It was estimated that her body had been there for three weeks. Born in Arizona October 20, 1949, she had been missing since November 9.

With more and more bodies turning up, a task force was formed to catch the predator, now dubbed The Hillside Strangler. The task force was initially composed of 30 officers from the Los Angeles Police Department, the Sheriff's Department and the Glendale Police Department. The cousins soon struck again, claiming their tenth victim, Lauren Rae Wagner. The 18-year-old business student at Mondore High School lived with her parents in the San Fernando Valley, in the hills around Glendale's Mount Washington. The couple had retired to bed, fully expecting their daughter to be home before midnight. The next morning, they saw her car parked across the street and the door had been left ajar. When her father questioned neighbours to see if they could shed any light on their daughter's whereabouts, Beulah Stofer said she had seen Lauren pull over in her car at about 9pm. A car with two men then pulled up beside her. One of them was tall and young, and the other was older and shorter with bushy hair. Some sort of disagreement ensued and Stofer heard Wagner cry out 'You won't get away with this!' She then ended up in the other car. Her body was found on November 29 on the west side of Mount Washington at 1217 Cliff Drive in Glassell Park, with ligature marks on her neck, ankles and wrists. She also had burn marks on her hands, leading investigators to believe she had been tortured.

Eleven days before Christmas, the body of 17-year-old prostitute Kimberly Diane Martin was discovered on a deserted lot near Los Angeles City Hall, located at the centre of City Hall Park in the Civic Centre area of Lower Manhattan, between Broadway, Park Row and Chambers Street. Fearing for her life on the streets with a killer loose, Martin had taken the precaution of joining the Climax call girl agency. Tragically, the killer cousins placed a call to that same agency from a payphone in the lobby of the Hollywood Public Library on Ivar Street and she was despatched. When police later attended apartment 114 at 1950 Tamarind, where she had been sent, it was vacant but had been broken into.

The 13th and final victim in the cousins' horrendous killing spree was 21-year-old Cindy Lee Hudspeth, who was murdered on February 16, 1978. The popular, vivacious young woman had dreams of making enough money to attend college by giving dance lessons. She was last seen in her apartment building at 800 E. Garfield Avenue, from where she presumably headed towards Glendale Community College, where she worked nights answering the telephone. Somewhere between home and college, she was kidnapped. As it transpired, she lived just across the street from Kristina Weckler, another victim, although they did not know each other. Having been strangled and mutilated, Hudspeth's body was placed in the trunk of her Datsun and pushed off a cliff on Angeles Crest Highway, a two-lane highway that runs over the San Gabriel Mountains in Los Angeles County. A helicopter pilot had spotted the seemingly abandoned orange Datsun on February 17. The police response team attending the wreck discovered the body in the boot of the vehicle. It showed ligature marks, and she had been raped, tortured and strangled.

Then... nothing—the killings stopped. The authorities were at a loss, and with a lack of further victims, the Hillside Strangler Task Force was disbanded shortly after Cindy Lee's murder. On April 1, 1978, the Washington Post reported that the bizarre case of the Hillside Strangler may have been transformed into the even stranger Case of the Hillside Stranglings: a Beverly Hills handyman and convicted Boston bank robber, Peter Jones, was arrested on suspicion of murdering Kathleen Robinson and Jill Barcomb, two of the women listed as among the strangler's victims. Daryl Gates, the recently installed police chief, had headed the 92-member Hillside Strangler Task Force prior to his appointment. He stated that information received from George Francis Shamshak, a 27-year-old Massachusetts convict serving a four-year term for bank robbery, had implicated both himself and Jones in two killings, and claimed it as a major breakthrough. Shamshak and Jones had been boyhood friends from the working-class Roxbury section of Boston and briefly roomed together. The police stated that Jones was not a suspect in 11 of the 13 strangler killings, and Shamshak was in prison when three of them were committed. Also, neither man fitted composite drawings made of two men who drove off with one of the victims in the December.

The investigators, of course, were well accustomed to prisoners making false accusations, so they brought along their lie detector. Shamshak convinced them that he was talking about actual crimes, and officers duly reported their findings to their colleagues in Los Angeles. In statements made to Massachusetts-based investigators, Shamshak said Jones claimed to have hit one of the women on the head with a blunt instrument. He also reportedly said that Jones strangled one victim and stabbed another. The problem with that claim was that there had been no record of any victim having been stabbed. According to the report in the Washington Post, some of the Hollywood prostitutes who'd been friends of the victims had scoffed from the very beginning at the theory of a single strangler being responsible. The police had linked the crimes because of the method of killing and because the victims had been mutilated in a way which they refused to disclose. Three days later the New York Times reported that 36-year-old Peter Jones had been released because of lack of evidence against him. While Jones had been under interrogation, he maintained his innocence. 'We have been unable to find evidence to support Shamshak's story and at this time it would be highly improper to hold Mr Jones in custody,' Gates told a news conference.

Sensationalist reporting in the tabloid media had brought the full glare of the intensive manhunt for The Hillside Strangler to the public's attention, and general panic penetrated the neighbourhoods. Meanwhile, Bianchi had continued applying for law enforcement jobs, even during his killing rampage, and had made acquaintances in the LAPD. He even occasionally accompanied officers on ride-alongs through the city's streets as officers scouted for the killers. When he told his cousin about it, Buono flew into a rage, particularly when Bianchi said he'd been questioned in relation to the Hillside Strangler case. Furious Buono threatened to kill him if he didn't get out of town. Bianchi reunited with Kelly Boyd, his girlfriend and mother of his son, Sean. Following the birth Kelly had relocated to Bellingham in Washington State and when Bianchi joined them, they fell quickly into a family routine. Bianchi took a job as a security guard, earning the trust of his colleagues. He had escaped Hollywood's bright lights and the media frenzy, but it wasn't long before his murderous tendencies caused his downfall.

The fear spreading through Los Angeles ratcheted up another notch when Bianchi struck again, murdering two university students in the same day. It was the evening of January 11, 1979, when 22-year-old student Karen Mandic and her friend, 27-year-old Diane Wilder, arrived to house-sit for an acquaintance of theirs, a certain Kenneth Bianchi. Early the following morning, Bellingham Police Department received information from a security office at Western Washington University (WWU) that two students were missing. Wilder was a transfer student, majoring in dance, at WWU's Fairhaven College, and Mandic was a junior, majoring in business administration. They shared a rental house at 1246 Ellis Street. Mandic clerked part-time at Fred Meyer Super Shopping Centre to supplement money she received from her parents for her education. Although it was supposed to be a secret, Mandic had told co-workers and friends that she and Wilder had been offered $100 each by Kenneth Bianchi, from Whatcom Security, to guard a residence in the secluded Edgemoor neighbourhood for two hours while the security alarm system was being repaired. Located at 334 Bayside Road, it was a sprawling, ranch-style house, overlooking Chuckanut Bay and owned by William Catlow, a recently retired Georgia-Pacific Corporation executive, who was holidaying in Europe with his wife, Cleora. Later that evening, Karen's friend Steve Hardwick, concerned that he had not heard from her, called the police. Having initially interviewed Bianchi, the authorities then went to the house the young women shared. Shortly after 4.30pm on the following day, their bodies were found in Mandic's car. Both had been strangled. The police discovered a piece of paper in the car which detailed the meeting with Bianchi. Hauling him in for questioning, it was not long before they knew they had their man–painstaking forensic analysis of the car and Bianchi's home tied him indisputably to the murders. It was only then that links to the Strangler case began to fall into place.

On March 21, 1979, as he was being prepared for trial, Bianchi was hypnotised and turned into 'Steve', a foul-mouthed braggart who boasted of the Los Angeles and Bellingham murders. He also claimed he had a partner in crime, his cousin Angelo Buono, a petty criminal with an oversized ego. Bianchi said: '(Angelo) may have been a criminal years ago... none of us are perfect.' Buono was arrested but vehemently proclaimed his innocence, saying he had absolutely nothing to do with any of the murders. In October 1979, Bianchi pleaded guilty to the Bellingham killings. Taken to Los Angeles, he then pleaded guilty to five more murders. Meanwhile, following his arrest, Buono was charged with 10 murders. Fabricating an insanity defence, Bianchi stated he had dissociative identity disorder and a personality separate from himself had committed the murders. Court psychologists, notably Dr Martin Orne, observed Bianchi and deemed him to be faking the condition. Bianchi eventually pleaded guilty to the Washington murders and five of the murders in California, testifying against Buono to avoid the death penalty. Buono, as the accused accomplice of a defendant who'd already confessed, pleaded innocent to the 10 counts of murder against him. He thought he had the case won, citing a lack of any physical evidence linking him to the murders. With hundreds of witnesses eventually turning up to testify against him, it was a far cry from the fact that he initially thought his cousin's testimony was the only thing that the prosecution had against him. At a preliminary hearing held on July 6, 1981, Bianchi testified that he did not know if he'd been telling the truth when he told the police of Buono's involvement. In light of this unexpected statement, Buono's attorney, Roger Kelly, moved to dismiss all 10 counts of murder against his client. On July 21, Judge Ronald M George, the appointed judge for the Buono case, denied Kelly's motion, explaining that a dismissal would not be 'in the furtherance of justice.' That same year the District Attorney's office withdrew from Buono's case and Attorney General George Deuk-mejian brought in two new attorneys for the prosecution, Michael Nash and Michael Boren. Paul Tulleners, a special investigator, was assigned to assist them in evaluating the evidence. After deciding that the evidence against Buono was sufficient enough to prosecute, it was decided that George Deukmejian would act for the prosecution.

Angelo Buono's case finally went to trial on November 16, 1981, but was immediately disrupted by continuances, which the defence appealed all the way to the California Supreme Court. The actual trial finally began in the spring of 1982, after jury selection took three-and-a-half months to complete. What followed was the most expensive trial in the history of the California legal system at that time. It continued for more than a year, involving 392 witnesses and 56,000 pages of testimony. Several of the witnesses were girls Buono had abused and tormented, including Becky Spears and Sabra Hannan. The judge and jury were taken to the hillsides where the victims were found and given a presentation by the key detective at each site. The prosecution then produced a key witness, a young girl whom Buono had a run-in with on the night he and Bianchi murdered 17-year-old Kimberly Diane Martin. She told the court that Buono had harassed and terrorised her in Hollywood Public Library in Lower Manhattan, and testified that Buono used a payphone there to ring the Climax call girl agency, calls which investigators were never able to link to any one person at the time.

On October 21, 1983, the jury began their deliberations. Ten days later, they found Buono not guilty of murdering Yolanda Washington but guilty of murdering Judy Miller, Dolores Cepeda, Sonja Johnson, Kimberly Martin, Kristina Weckler, Lisa Kastin, Jane King and Cindy Hudspeth. Taking the stand after the jury's deliberations, Buono claimed: 'My morals and constitutional rights have been broken.' The jury recommended life imprisonment, sparing him the death penalty. The judge upheld the sentence and Buono was initially sent to Folsom Prison, where he refused to come out of his cell for fear of being attacked by inmates. He was later transferred to Calipatria State Prison in California. At the conclusion of the trial, Judge George, who would later become Chief Justice of the California Supreme Court, said he would not have had the slightest reluctance to impose the death penalty in the case were it within his power to do so: 'Ironically, although these two defendants utilised almost every form of legalised execution against their victims, the defendants have escaped any form of capital punishment. Angelo Buono and Kenneth Bianchi slowly squeezed out of their victims their last breath of air and their promise for a future life. And all for what? The momentary sadistic thrill of enjoying a brief perverted sexual satisfaction and the venting of their hatred for women. If ever there was a case where the death penalty is appropriate, this is the case.'

In 1980 during the lead-up to his trial and from behind bars, Bianchi began a relationship with actress and playwright Veronica Lynn Chapman, who had an obsession with serial killers. She had written a screenplay about a female serial killer entitled The Mutilated Cutter, which she sent to Bianchi for his opinion. Bianchi manipulated Chapman into copycatting a Hillside Strangler murder to make it look like the killer was still at large and the wrong man had been sent to prison. Bianchi had given her some semen to use, smuggled out of prison in a rubber glove, to make it appear like a rape and murder committed by the Hillside Strangler. DNA evidence had no forensic use at the time, but semen could be analysed to show what blood type the man had. She lured a woman to a motel and attempted to strangle her. Fortunately, Chapman was overpowered and arrested, and jailed. She was released in 2003.

On March 24, 1986 and while in prison, Buono married 35-year-old mother of three Christine Kizuka, a supervisor at the Los Angeles office of the California State Department of Employee Development. They met when Kizuka visited her ex-husband in an adjacent cell to Buono, serving a term for assault with a deadly weapon. She began visiting Buono, although prison officials agreed to never allow conjugal visits between them due to the nature of Buono's crimes and his history of violence against the opposite sex. 'I want to emphasise that Buono has never had a conjugal visit. He is not recommended to ever have a conjugal visit... due to the nature of his crimes against women,' stated Department of Corrections spokesman Bob Gore. But inmates were allowed to marry, and The Los Angeles Herald Examiner reported that Buono and Kizuka wed in a five-minute civil ceremony, conducted by corrections official Richard Wipf in a visiting area at Folsom Prison. Wipf commented that it was 'just a routine marriage. They were both happy.' Ms Kizuka and her lawyer declined to comment to the newspaper, but acquaintances reported that the marriage had been kept a secret from her family. This was Buono's fourth marriage. His third had ended three months after his conviction. Six years later he was dead, having suffered a heart attack on September 21, 2002, at Calipatria State Prison. He was alone in his cell at the time.

Meanwhile, in September 23, 1989, the Los Angeles Times reported that Bianchi had married a Louisiana pen pal the same week as meeting her for the first time. He wore a black tuxedo during the 15-minute the ceremony in the prison chapel. Shirlee Joyce Book, 36, of Monterey, wore a white wedding dress with a small veil, according to Richard Bauer, a Washington State Penitentiary spokesman.

In a strange twist of fate, in 2007, Buono's grandson Christopher shot his grandmother, Mary Castillo, in the head and upper body. Castillo was one of Buono's four wives, and had five children to him, including Chris's father. According to a report in the Los Angeles Times on January 20 written by David Haldane, Christopher Buono, of Fullerton, died at about 11.15am at Yorba Linda Patio and Hearth, in the 3900 block of Prospect Avenue, after shooting 67-year-old Castillo. He had taken his own life. Castillo was taken to an undisclosed hospital for treatment. Rachanee Srisavasdi reported in the Orange County Register that Christopher had been in the storage space of Yorba Linda Patio and Hearth when he shot her. His father apparently owned the storage space, and police said the motive was unknown. 'I don't understand why he did what he did,' a neighbor was quoted as saying. 'She had nothing to do with (what Angelo Buono) did, she concentrated on raising her children. People should leave her alone, or care about her because she's Mary, not because she used to be married to that man.'

Washington State Penitentiary is a Washington State Department of Corrections men's prison located in Walla Walla. With an operating capacity of 2,200, it is the second largest prison in the state and is where Kenneth Bianchi is currently serving time. Having received six life sentences on January 4, 1984, his most recent request for parole in 2010 was denied by a state board in Sacramento, according to Los Angeles County district attorney's office spokeswoman Sandi Gibbons. Bianchi will be eligible to apply for parole again in 2025, so in the meantime he will have plenty of time to look at the wheat fields surrounding the prison and reflect on his heinous crimes.

CHAPTER 6

JAMES WARREN JONES

INSTIGATOR OF THE JONESTOWN
MASS MURDER-SUICIDE

'I love socialism, and I'm willing to die to bring it about, but if I did, I'd take a thousand with me.'—Reverend Jim Jones, religious cult leader and civil rights activist.

TAKING A leap of faith is a harmless enough saying. One is perceived as being optimistic about one's actions, and that they will transpire to be prosperous ones. But look upon it in a negative sense, and the phrase can take on far more disturbing connotations, in that one can ignore facts, perceptions or odds against them and go somewhat blindly ahead anyway, believing that things will be better.

The Danish philosopher, theologian and cultural critic Soren Aabye Kierkegaard argued that life was only worth living if one had total faith in God. He also made a distinction between belief and faith. Belief is trust in something which is supported by evidence. Faith is trust in the face of no logical support or tangible evidence. When we head out on the search for identity, it can often lead us to the precipice of blind faith, when there is little choice but to prepare for a fall. There is no time, or need, to think, just desperation to act. It is just those desperate acts of blind faith that can have both dire and tragic consequences. All too often we learn about what happens when people close their eyes to the world and instead listen to the curated arguments of one leader, one spiritual guide, manipulated and motivated by an ill-conceived grab at salvation, which is often then triggered into a course of violent action.

There is one word that springs to mind when considering a learned response to a particular person, stimuli or trigger, and that is conditioning. While it comes across as a harmless and neutral process, conditioning can also be brought into play to influence in bad or nefarious ways. Collective hallucination, psychological games and loyalty tests all work towards sapping free will and tap into primal fears, mangling beliefs so that one has a need to belong to a group, a people, a cause, a cult. Almost anyone vulnerable or with impaired judgement is at risk of becoming sucked into a 'family'. Perhaps the most notorious family ever to have existed was that run by cult leader Charles Manson at Spahn Ranch, located in Death Valley National Park in eastern California. In the late 1960s, Manson weaved together beliefs drawn partly from Satanism and Scientology, touting race war and murder: all actions focussed against societal law. Through mystical manipulation, Manson demanded unquestioning loyalty. And then there are cult suicides, perhaps the most terrifying aspect of what can happen within a religion. Little wonder, then, that the word cult is commonly used to denote a dangerous or destructive religion, because mass suicide is by its very nature destructive. Mass suicides are most often undertaken by groups that feel trapped within circumstances they cannot control or escape from other than through death. History speaks of events where groups of Jews have killed themselves (or each other, as suicide is strongly condemned in Judaism) to escape torture, painful execution such as burning, or slavery, such as the siege of Masada by Roman troops at the end of the First Jewish-Roman War, which ended in the mass suicide of 960 people on a hilltop overlooking the Dead Sea in present-day Israel.

Almost as many people died at a religious commune in Guyana in 1978. The jungle commune, known as Jonestown after the group's leader Jim Jones, was also known as the People's Temple. The people living there had fled from San Francisco through fear of persecution from authorities and the media who wanted to investigate the treatment of some of the commune's members. The mass suicide occurred shortly after U.S. congressman Leo Ryan visited Jonestown accompanied by a couple of staffers, news reporters and relatives of some of those in the commune. Ryan travelled to Guyana to address claims that some members were being held against their will. By all accounts acting on orders from Jones, the visitors were attacked at Port Kaituma airport as they prepared to depart for home. Nine people were injured and six died, including Ryan, who remains the only member of congress to die in the line of duty. It was then that Jones urged his community to die with dignity rather than submit to the capitalist forces he saw as their enemy. Some suicides were voluntary, but many were forced at gunpoint to drink poison and those who attempted to flee were shot. Jones was among the dead. In all, 909 individuals died, all but two from apparent cyanide poisoning, in an event termed 'revolutionary suicide' by Jones and some People's Temple members, captured on an audiotape recording.

James Warren Jones was born on May 13, 1931 in Crete, three miles east of the town of Lynn, Indiana, to disabled First World War veteran James Thurman Jones, who had suffered from exposure to mustard gas in France, and Lynetta Jones, née Putnam. College educated and ambitious, Lynetta worked in a variety of jobs and as a result, her son was often left to care for himself. His alcoholic father, meanwhile, was a mystic fortune-teller and paid his son little attention. Young Jones would visit the town library and churches and was occasionally encouraged to read from the scriptures to enthralled congregations. Myrtle Kennedy, a friend of his mother, lived nearby and ensured that the boy attended Sunday school, giving him instruction in the Bible. By the age of 10, Jones was well into his religious quest and under the spell of a woman evangelist and the leader of faith-healing revivals at the Gospel Tabernacle Church, a charismatic, Pentecostal sect of 'Holy Rollers' who believed in faith healing. It was during this time that Jones suffered the onset of nightmares and was terrorised by dreams in which a snake figured prominently. As a child, he was heavily influenced by the works of Karl Marx, Joseph Stalin, Adolf Hitler and Mahatma Gandhi. Such was his passion for the church that he would absorb what he learned at different houses of worship and impart this knowledge to other children in the community. Despite his liking for the spoken word, he had few friends to speak of, possibly because he alienated many due to his religious zest, seeing dancing and drinking as sinful pastimes. Jones grew up intolerant of the racial discrimination seen in America, possibly because of his own experiences as an outcast. On one occasion he clashed with his father when he did not allow his son's black friend to enter the house.

When his parents separated in 1948, Jones moved with his mother to Richmond, a city in east central Indiana, bordering Ohio. Entering high school, he cultivated a reputation as a thick-skulled intellectual who usually insisted his ideas were correct and who frequently exerted his will upon his peers, as if testing his power. It was while working as a hospital orderly that Jones met Marceline Baldwin, an older nursing student. After graduating early from high school in December 1948, Jones started at Indiana University the following month. He was a16-year-old freshman living at what is now the Ashton Center at IU, and married

Marceline after his first term on June 12, 1949. The couple eventually adopted several children, some of whom were non-white. He referred to them as his 'rainbow family' and would later use the term in reference to his religious followers. At IU, Jones was seen as a loner. He would sit alone, staring into the Jordan River that ran through the campus, often for hours at a time. The Jordan is actually categorised as a natural stream, not a river, where its waters come from natural springs, surface run-off and storm drains. Whatever its categorisation, it was clearly somewhere that the young Jones found peace and tranquillity. Kenneth Lemons, Jones's freshman roommate, would state in an Indiana Daily Student article nine days after the Jonestown massacre that everyone got on beautifully—except for Jones. 'This man had not one friend in the dormitory from the time he moved in until he moved out. But he wanted it that way,' he said. He was not surprised by the news of Jones's cult, as he had viewed himself as somewhat of a messiah. Lemons also said in a Herald Times article at around the same time that Jones showed radical religious and political views while at school. 'He considered himself above everyone else and pored over the Bible, often rambling about his religious philosophies,' said Lemon.

During his time as an undergraduate at IU, Jones never declared a major. In May 1951 he moved with his wife to Indianapolis, where he resumed schooling during the spring semester of 1953 at IU Indianapolis, but again never completed an undergraduate degree. Attending night school at Butler University, he earned a degree in secondary education in 1961, 10 years after first enrolling. Jones had taken a hiatus until 1959, during which time he founded what would become the People's Temple Christian Church Full Gospel. In 1951 he began attending meetings of the Communist party in Indianapolis. Agitated by open communists in the USA, he would ask himself: 'How can I demonstrate my Marxism? The thought was to infiltrate the church.' After years of struggling to find his way, in 1952 Jones announced he was entering the ministry, and a Methodist superintendent helped him get just the start he was hoping for.

He became a student pastor in the Somerset Southside Methodist Church in a poor, predominantly white neighbourhood in Indianapolis. He observed that people with money were attracted to faith healing, and soon realised that such services offered financial resources which could prove helpful to his own goals. By the following year, having made his 'evangelical debut' at a ministerial seminar in Detroit, Michigan, he was earning a reputation as a healer and evangelist. He was holding racially integrated services, an interest not shared by his church. The church once stood at 3230 S. Keystone Avenue, and he and Marceline lived nearby in the 3000 block of Villa Avenue. The church is no more, having made way for a petrol station and convenience store.

By 1954, Jones had established the Community Unity Church in Indianapolis, while preaching also at the Laurel Tabernacle. To raise money, he formulated the extraordinary idea to import monkeys from Calcutta, India. The plan was to sell them door-to-door as pets for $29 each. His plan worked, and he used this as an incentive to grow his congregation by periodically awarding the imported animals to church members who brought in the highest numbers of new members. He later credited his monkey strategy as growing his flock to about 300 people. Despite its initial success, the scheme began to unravel when monkeys started arriving dead. In April 1954, only one monkey of a shipment of three survived. The following week three out of seven monkeys were barely alive. When he received a $89 air freight bill, based on seven monkeys, he abandoned them in the customs warehouse in the basement of the Federal Building. Assistant Customs Collector Eugene J. Okon came to the distressed monkeys' aid. Having despatched someone to buy a bunch of bananas, he then mixed the fruit with some brandy he'd confiscated, and the strange concoction was fed to the monkeys. According to a report in the Indianapolis Star, an hour later the three animals were able to sit up and chatter softly among themselves.

Jones's burgeoning notoriety took another turn when he pressed his church to allow African-Americans to attend services, which they resisted mightily, eventually forcing him to find a new congregation. Jones spent a short time as an associate minister at Laurel Street Tabernacle near Fountain Square, gathering the first few members of what would become the People's Temple. He also occasionally took to the pulpit of the church at St. Clair and Park Avenue, in what is today the Phoenix Theatre. Later, in 1954 and utilising the profits from his monkey sales, Jones opened the first inter-racial church in Indianapolis, at Hoyt Avenue and Randolph Street, called Wings of Deliverance. To build his following, Jones bought airtime on a local AM radio station to broadcast sermons. As a young preacher he captivated followers with his Pentecostal-influenced theatrics and staged faith healings.

By 1956, Jones had fully established the Wings of Deliverance Church as a successor to Community Unity. He bought his first church, a modest, wooden-framed building in the racially mixed Old Northside of Indianapolis at 1506 North New Jersey Street. He renamed it the People's Temple Full Gospel Church but almost immediately it was christened as the People's Temple. The inspiration for its new name stemmed from the fact that the church was housed in what was formerly a Jewish synagogue, a 'temple' Jones had purchased with little or no money down, for $50,000. Ironically, the man who aided the start of the People's Temple was the Rabbi Maurice Davis, a prominent anti-cult activist and sometime 'deprogrammer' who sold the synagogue to Jones on such remarkably generous terms. Around the mid-1950s a number of churches were promoting healings, with a small number even guaranteeing miracles. This was an opportunity too good to miss for Jones, who was then claiming to perform healings on a regular basis. One newspaper advert published on April 9, 1955 stated: '51 converted and healed last Sun.' Jones's ads would take it to extremes, claiming in one published on April 2,

1955: '1,000 Definite Testimonies of Healing Miracles in this City.' Despite the outlandish statements, some good came out of the People's Temple. Under Jones's guidance, soup kitchens were held alongside canned food drives for the city's poor, as well as campaigns for racial equality in the former hotbed of the Ku Klux Klan. Jones was happy to practice what he preached as he and Marceline created their rainbow family. The couple adopted three children of Korean-American ancestry named Law, Suzanne and Stephanie. In 1954 they adopted Agnes Jones, an 11-year-old girl of Native American ancestry. In 1959 the couple had their first and only biological child, Stephan Gandhi Jones. Two years later they adopted James Warren Jr., becoming the first white couple in America to adopt a black child. They then adopted another son and called him Jim Jones.

In 1960, Indianapolis' 35th Mayor, Charles Boswell, appointed Jones as director of the Human Rights Commission, and he helped desegregate churches, restaurants, theatres, the Riverside Amusement Park and the Methodist Hospital, work he was lauded for by the Indianapolis Recorder, the city's African-American newspaper. For more than 60 years, Riverside Amusement Park sat adjacent to Riverside City Park at 30th Street between the White River and the Central Canal. It was established in 1902 by Frederick Ingersoll, of the Pittsburgh Construction Company, and three Indianapolis entrepreneurs. The location was unique and the regional park drew many visitors looking to escape the hustle and bustle of city life, visit animals at an early version of a local zoo, or play golf on one of the three public courses that sprang up between 1900 and 1904. With more rides and entertainment added, Riverside saw a surge in attendance shortly after the Second World War, but attendance was affected by the rise in popularity of the family car. While the swimming and boating facilities remained popular, ides began to fall into disrepair and required costly improvements.

The park's white-only policy marked an embarrassing chapter in the city's history; it was open to non-white patrons on infrequent Coloured Frolic Days. Following protests, in 1964 the park changed its admission policy to allow 'minority' visitors, but it never fully recovered from the controversy and it closed at the end of the 1970 season.

Conservative Democratic Mayor Boswell made $7,000 available to fund the city's Human Rights Commission directorship. Advertising the job by word of mouth, the selection committee had only one applicant. In the resultant job interview at City Hall, the committee—a rabbi, a black judge and a priest—appraised Jim Jones without carrying out a background check. They were unaware of his healings, although they had seen his name on the religious pages of the newspaper and knew him as an advocate of the poor and black people. Jones was an articulate and humane 'eager beaver' social worker, though he put off the priest a little by flaunting his fundamentalist Protestantism. After the interview, the committee duly recommended their only candidate to the Mayor, who made the appointment because the post had to be filled. Boswell instructed Jones to keep a low profile, proceed diplomatically and avoid inflaming the racial climate or antagonising the business community. The position was a golden opportunity for Jones to gain access to new forums for his views, via radio and television, and in public appearances. He capitalised on the highly newsworthy topic of race relations while increasing his own visibility tenfold. He'd been in the job less than two months when the Mayor and several commissioners ordered him to slow down on his 'journalistic efforts', clearly concerned that he was showing a counter-productive appetite for publicity in a delicate area. Despite the admonishment, Jones, with his typical crusader's bent, continued to shout his principles, often with rhetoric more militant than his actions. He served as an active commissioner for more than a year until he suddenly relocated with his family to Belo Horizonte, the capital city of south-eastern Brazil's Minas Gerais state, in 1962.

On April 11, 1962, the Jones family stepped off a commercial flight at Sao Paulo and travelled to Belo Horizonte, checking in at the expensive Financial Hotel. They then moved into a large house at 203 Maraba Avenue in the city's prosperous Santo Antonia section where, according to neighbour Sebastiaco Carlos Rocha, they enjoyed an expensive lifestyle. Somewhat mysteriously, Jones would leave the house early each morning carrying a suitcase and return at around six or seven in the evening, never explaining where he'd been, what he was doing or what he was carrying.

According to Rocha, his new neighbour said he was a retired U.S. Navy captain and was in Brazil to recuperate from the Korean War, which had ended nine years before.

In an interview with the San Jose Mercury News in November 1978, Rocha said his neighbour was mostly uncommunicative but when he did talk, he tended to ramble. Jones, he said, enjoyed talking about war in general and displayed a preoccupation with the world's social ills, and hated hearing anything bad about black people, or people in general. Jones also told Rocha that he received a monthly payment from the U.S. Government for his military service. Rocha's wife, Elza, a lawyer in Belo Horizonte, recalled that Jones said he had a city job at Eureka Laundries—a claim denied by Sebastian Dias de Magalhaes, head of Industrial Relations for Eureka in 1962. Dias and two other Eureka employees later said Jones lied to conceal what they believed was his work for the CIA. Jones attended a church operated by American Pentecostal missionaries in a suburb of the city, where he became argumentative with the missionaries. According to other neighbours anonymously quoted in the San Jose Mercury News article, Jones's daughter Suzanne said her father intended to establish a branch of his People's Temple in Brazil.

According to Jones's main biographer, Tim Reiterman, Jones supplemented his income by becoming a gigolo, engaging in sex with women in exchange for donations to an orphanage where he worked, all with the consent of his wife. The scenario that Reiterman portrayed came mainly from Jones's own account of his stay in Brazil, and there is no evidence to substantiate his claim. Meanwhile, Jones's church back home in the U.S. was not fairing so well financially. Congregation numbers tumbled as the regulars felt abandoned by their travelling pastor.

In mid-December 1962, Jones moved 250 miles west to Rio de Janeiro, where he and his family resided at 154 Rua Senador Vigueiro in the Flamengo neighbourhood. According to the Brazil Herald on December 24-26, 1978, Jones found a job as an investment salesman on a commission-only basis for the American-owned Invesco S.A. He didn't sell anything in the three months he worked there. The family were in Brazil on temporary visas, good for eleven months only. Brazilian immigration authorities said Jones left Rio for an unknown country at the end of March 1963, and never returned. In fact, Jones returned to Indianapolis and the sanctuary of his church, by now called the People's Temple Full Gospel Church and affiliated with the Disciples of Christ, for which Jones was ordained as a minister in 1964. Administering to his congregation, Jones gave an impassioned speech about how the world would be engulfed by a nuclear war on July 15, 1967, and from the ashes would rise a socialist Eden on Earth. Riding on the back of his sermon, Jones said the Temple had to move to Northern California for safety.

He had pinpointed the Mendocino County region, which he had read in an Esquire magazine article as being a nuclear-safe zone. In 1964 Jones duly moved with about a hundred members of his faithful flock to Redwood Valley, 100 miles north of San Francisco.

'Ukiah Welcomes New Citizens to Community' declared a local newspaper on July 26, 1965. It was accompanied by a photograph of a clean-cut Jones posing alongside his wife and four children. The article went on to describe the People's Temple Christian Church of the Disciples of Christ as gathering around a central, controversial idea, 'that all men—white, black, yellow or red—are one brotherhood'. To the mostly white farming community of Mendocino County, it was a rude awakening to a burgeoning, radical doomsday cult borne from racial tensions and seismic changes. Jones taught pupils in Redwood Valley, Potter Valley and Boon-eville, as well as covering night classes at the Ukiah Adult School, and was popular in class.

Pressure was placed on the children of Temple members to obtain good grades, and members themselves were required to understand the importance of the political process and voting, as Jones sermonised on patriotism. It was not all good times, however, as the Temple came under harassment from local agitators and white supremacists, who called members 'nigger lovers.' On one occasion Jones was verbally accosted while in the pulpit and threatened with a knife. Such was the escalation in threats that Temple members started toting guns. Despite this, Jones continued his doctrine against traditional Christianity and the Temple began to grow, with branches springing up in numerous cities. As far as Jones was concerned, his way was the only way and tragically, brainwashed followers believed him. 'If you see me as your friend, I'll be your friend,' he once said. 'As you see me as your father, I'll be your father, for those of you that don't have a father … If you see me as your saviour, I'll be your saviour. If you see me as your God, I'll be your God.'

In 1973 Jones prepared a contingency plan to escape from detractors. Five-hundred members would construct 'Jonestown', a self-sustaining agricultural commune in the African country of Guyana and a sanctuary from rising media scrutiny. The move could not come soon enough for Jones, because of an impending exposé of allegations of abuse by former Temple members. Come the summer of 1977, several hundred from his evangelical flock uprooted their Californian lives and moved with their self-proclaimed messiah to the remote jungle location to join original settlers. But what had once been a nicely settled community suddenly found itself in a propaganda war; Jones launched into lengthy, often communist-slanted monologues. It was a miserable existence, working under enforced prison camp-like rules, with little food to speak of and daily assaults by mosquitos. Work and study were the order of the day as Jones ranted on about CIA invasions and capitalist pigs set on destroying their colony, all the while testing his followers' loyalty to the cause. Some understandably wanted out but it was not easy; they were told there were spies in the camp ready and willing to denounce planned defectors. There was neither trust nor solidarity—Jonestown was slowly unravelling.

Back in the U.S., Jonestown came to the attention of California congressman Leo Ryan. Some of his constituents' relatives were at the commune, and they were concerned that they were being held against their will. His resolve was hardened by an affidavit from Deborah Layton Blakey, a former Jones aide who had managed to seek refuge at the American Embassy and recounted exactly what was happening at Jonestown. Ryan wrote to Jones requesting an invitation to the settlement. At first, Jones declined but later acquiesced, so Ryan travelled to Guyana with some of the relatives and a media crew.

On the afternoon of Friday, November 17, escorted by Richard Dwyer, Deputy Chief of Mission at the U.S. Embassy, Ryan and part of his contingent were given a tour of the commune. Food and a place to sleep had been arranged by Temple attorneys Charles Garry and Mark Lane. Jones was well prepared for the visit and had primed his followers who had, in turn, been primed by Jones's loyal lieutenants to fabricate living conditions. Ryan's party met Jones and also spoke with the organisation's rank-and-file. By Saturday afternoon, all was going well. Ryan was speaking favourably of several aspects of the settlement when a note was smuggled to Ryan's aide, asking for help. Several defectors declared themselves, saying they wanted to leave under the congressman's protection. As Ryan and his team prepared to leave the settlement with 14 defectors in tow for an airstrip at nearby Port Kaituma, a knife-wielding man attacked him. The incident was quickly dealt with, and

Ryan was unharmed. Even so, it brought a sudden end to the uneasy truce that had prevailed in the previous 24 hours.

Having reached the airstrip in time for their 4.30pm return flight on November 18, Ryan had expected two planes to be waiting but there were none on the ground. The planes showed up about 40 minutes later and as the first plane taxied, Temple member Larry Layton took out a handgun and began firing at his fellow passengers. He wounded several before he was overpowered. As the remaining passengers boarded the second aircraft, a tractor and trailer pulled up, and Temple members fired shotguns, handguns and rifles at the departing group. Ryan was shot more than 20 times and did not survive. Three members of the media and a defector were also killed, and many others injured. Some of the group fled into the surrounding jungle, hiding from sight and tending to each other's wounds. As the Jonestown death squad returned to camp, one of the planes—its engine damaged—took off for the capital, its crew carrying news of the ambush. As night descended on western Guyana, the stranded visitors concealed themselves in a rum shop at Port Kaituma to await evacuation the following morning. But another tragedy was about to unfold.

A mere five miles away, Jones was told what had happened at the airstrip. In return, he told his followers that it was time for them to transition to the other side—they must drink Flavour Aid laced with cyanide, and there was no escape. Surrounded by rows of guards armed with crossbows and guns, families were forced to take the drink and died together. Those who refused to drink were injected with cyanide instead. 'Die with a degree of dignity. Lay down your life with dignity; don't lay down with tears and agony,' said Jones in response to the outcry at being force-fed the poison. 'I tell you, I don't care how many screams you hear, I don't care how many anguished cries... death is a million times preferable to ten more days of this life. If you knew what was ahead of you—if you knew what was ahead of you, you'd be glad to be stepping over tonight.'

Guyanese defence forces arrived at the airstrip shortly after dawn the following day. They secured the runway and turned toward Jonestown, marching down the long, rough road to the commune. They were horrified to find almost 1,000 bodies spread across an area the size of a football field—innocent men, women and children lying dead in an arc around the settlement's central pavilion. Unbeknown to most Temple members, half-pound shipments of cyanide had been delivered to the commune every month since 1976 under Jones's orders, under the guise of using it to clean gold. Survivor Odell Rhodes later told the Washington Post that babies were the first to die. 'It just got all out of order,' he said, 'babies were screaming, children were screaming and there was mass confusion.' Just 87 people survived in all. The dead totalled 918. Jones died of a gunshot to the head, probably suicide. He was found between two other bodies, lying next to the chair from where he'd given speeches, his head cushioned by a pillow. Jonestown became the greatest single loss of American civilian life in a deliberate act until the 9/11 terror attack.

If it had not been for Jonestown, Guyana would possibly have remained South America's best-kept secret. The patch of rainforest which was home to the People's Temple has pretty much been reclaimed by the jungle. Search long and hard enough, and you may well stumble upon remnants of the colony. The metal drums in which Jones was known to have mixed his poisonous concoction are still in situ decades later. In 1983, Leo Ryan received a Congressional Gold Medal and in 2009, a post office in his old district of San Mateo, California, was named after him. 'Leo Ryan was the real deal,' said his former aide Jackie Speier, who was himself injured in the airstrip shooting. 'He carried around with him a righteous indignation and passion for the powerless of society and didn't shy away from questioning the status quo.

He didn't win all his battles, but to Leo, the fight was as important as the outcome.' While Jones's idiosyncratic blend of evangelical Christianity, New Age spirituality and radical social justice attracted an enthusiastic following, his members were later stereotyped as sinister, brainwashed idiots. Journalist Tim Reiterman argues in his seminal book Raven: The Untold Story of the Rev. Jim Jones and His People that many were 'decent, hardworking, socially conscious people, some highly educated', who 'wanted to help their fellow man and serve God, not embrace a self-proclaimed deity on earth'. Reiterman, at the time a journalist for the San Francisco Examiner, was one of the journalists attacked on the airstrip and survived two bullet wounds. In his 1980 study of Jonestown, writer Shiva Naipaul argued that the People's Temple was at its heart a fundamentalist religious project 'obsessed with sin and images of apocalyptic destruction, authoritarian in its innermost impulses, instinctively thinking in terms of the saved and the damned'. The result, Naipaul wrote, 'was neither racial justice nor socialism, but a messianic parody of both'.

Decades after the massacre at Jonestown, Jean Clancey, who worked on the Temple newspaper, recalled being part of a church and organisation to which members devoted a good portion of their lives, people 'who were capable of committing themselves to something outside of their own self-interests.' Laura Johnston Kohl, another former Temple member, said they were 'doing the right things, but in the wrong place with the wrong leader.' The biggest tragedy of Jonestown is that for most, they realised that too late.

CHAPTER 7

RODRIGO JACQUES ALCALA BUQUOR

THE DATING GAME KILLER

'This kind of case I have never experienced, and I hope to never again.'—Manhattan Criminal Court Judge Bonnie Wittner.

S AN ANTONIO in the early 1940s was like most 20th century American cities in the automotive age, its expansion mainly horizontal with sprawling neighbourhoods and little vertical construction. It was a place of change, where bohemian attitudes and attractions like the 'pansy craze' swept through the veins of society. New York and San Francisco were not the only cities laying claim to the exotic world of homosexuality, riding on the heels of the Harlem Renaissance. Exotic entertainment, courtesy of female impersonators, predominated at downtown venues, and morals violations and charges of indecent exposure were acted out in the courtroom.

As the gateway to the American southwest and the cradle of Texas liberty, the town was fast coming of age. No other city in Texas reflected the state's Mexican heritage better. Neither did the food. Tex-Mex first entered the English language as a nickname for the Texas Mexican Railway, which was charted in southern Texas in 1875. By the 1920s, the hyphenated form was being used in American newspapers to reference the railroad and describe Texans of Mexican ancestry. Most people today understand Tex-Mex as a cuisine influenced by cooking in the northern states of Mexico with the South Texas region between San Antonio, the Rio Grande Valley and El Paso. Beef, grilled food and tortillas, kid goat, barbecued beef heads and dried beef were common before Tex-Mex took on such Americanised elements as cheddar cheese, as goods from the U.S. became cheap and readily available.

Rodrigo Jacques Alcala Buquor was born on August 23, 1943, within the San Antonio sprawl to Anna Maria Gutierrez and Raoul Alcala Buquor. When he was eight, they and his two sisters and brother relocated across the border. Three years later, when Alcala was 11, his father abandoned them, so their mother took them to Los Angeles. In 1960, 17-year-old Alcala dropped out of school and enlisted in the U.S. Army, serving as a clerk for four years before he went AWOL and hitchhiked back to Los Angeles. He had been accused of sexual misconduct during his commission, and although the details of these accusations remain unclear, his erratic behaviour was attributed to some sort of nervous breakdown. After an evaluation by a military psychologist and an antisocial personality disorder diagnosis, Alcala was discharged on medical grounds in 1964.

As the premiere public arts school in the United States, the UCLA School of the Arts and Architecture in Los Angeles played a vital role in the cultural and artistic life of the campus and the broader community. Within its programmes, students have unparalleled opportunities to learn from and interact with a distinguished faculty who rank among the most accomplished artists, designers, architects, performers, ethnographers and scholars of our time. It was into this world that Alcala gravitated, earning a Bachelor of Fine Arts degree in 1968—the same year he kidnapped, raped, beat and tried to kill his first known victim. Hollywood was well in the throes of a renaissance, fired in the 1950s by the mushrooming television industry. Music recording studios were springing up and motion picture production was in full flight, with films including 2001: A Space Oddity, The Odd Couple and Bullit enjoying box office success. Riding on the wave of movie mania was a new generation of young filmmakers, influenced by the types of films produced, their production and marketing, and the way major studios approached filmmaking. The 'New Hollywood' period was one of revival, spurred on in part by the release of Bonnie and Clyde in 1967, with its combination of graphic violence and humour, linked to a theme of disaffected youth. The film represented a 'new cinema' through its blurred genre lines, and disregard for honoured aspects of plot and motivation. In both conception and execution, it was to prove a watershed picture. California was brimming with beautiful views and beautiful people. And it harboured a dark side in the form of Rodney Alcala.

Eight-year-old Tali Shapiro was walking along Sunset Boulevard when Alcala lured her into his car. The incident was witnessed by a passing motorist who followed the car, which didn't have licence plates, and called 911 to report the location. Police knocked on the door of Alcala's apartment. He answered and told them he was getting dressed. Officer Chris Camacho recalled: 'I will always remember that face at that door, very evil face.' Concerned for the girl's safety, the officers forced their way inside. Tali Shapiro was lying on the floor, naked and unconscious. She had been sexually abused and had a near-fatal head trauma, having been savagely beaten with a 10lb metal bar. Alcala escaped out of the back door. During a search of the apartment, pictures of young girls were discovered. They also found confirmation of Alcala's name and his attendance at UCLA. Armed with a rough description—about 5ft 6in to 6ft, about 140lb, with long brown curly hair—the search was on. Meanwhile, Tali and her family left the country. She was one of Alcala's only victims to survive. Decades later, she recalled the experience during one of Alcala's trials. She'd been wary when he'd pulled up, but Alcala told her he was a friend of her parents and had a beautiful picture to show her. Tali got into the car.

Alcala fled to New York, where he changed his name to John Berger and enrolled in New York University film school. For the next four years, he lived undetected, enjoying being a film student and amateur photographer under the tutelage of Roman Polanski, who taught him to use a camera. Polanski cemented his status in the film industry by directing Rosemary's Baby in 1968. His life took a tragic turn when his pregnant wife, Sharon Tate, was killed by members of the Charles Manson family in 1969. In 1977, he was arrested and charged with drugging and raping a 13-year-old girl, and subsequently pleaded guilty to the lesser offence of unlawful sex with a minor. Studying with Polanski later prompted Alcala to embark on a career as a self-proclaimed fashion photographer.

During the summer months, Alcala worked as a counsellor at an all-girl arts and drama camp in New Hampshire. In 1971, two girls attending the camp recognised Alcala on an FBI Most Wanted poster at the local post office. The police were alerted, and Alcala was arrested and extradited to California. But the prosecutor's case against him hit a roadblock. Tali Shapiro's family were in Mexico and refused to allow her to return to the U.S. to testify at the trial. With no main witness, Alcala was offered a plea deal. Sentenced to one year to life, he was paroled after 34 months under the indeterminate sentencing programme, which allowed a parole board, not a judge, to decide on when offenders are released, based on rehabilitation. The parole board believed artful, charming Alcala showed signs of rehabilitation, and he was back on the streets in less than three years.

Two months later, he was in prison again, having violated his parole for providing marijuana to a 13-year-old girl. She told the authorities that Alcala had kidnapped her, but no charge was forthcoming. He saw out two years behind bars before being released in 1977, once more under the indeterminate sentencing programme. Outside the prison walls, he returned to Los Angeles where he picked up a job as a typesetter for the Los Angeles Times. It was around this time that his interest in photography took a darker turn. Using his charm, he would lure young women and teenage boys and girls to his home to model for him, convincing many to pose nude, and amassed hundreds of photographs. Soon, he targeted his next assault victim, knocking 15-year-old hitchhiker Monique Hoyt unconscious and raping her. Thankfully Monique survived the ordeal. In November he struck again, this time escalating to murder. He attacked 18-year-old Jill Barcomb, a New Yorker who'd recently relocated. Using a large rock, Alcala smashed her face and strangled her to death by tying her belt and blue slacks around her neck. He dumped her body in a mountainous area in the foothills of Hollywood, in the vicinity of the famous sign. Her body was discovered on November 10, in a knee-to-chest position and naked from the waist down. She had been raped and sodomised and had three bite marks on her right breast.

Jill grew up on Park Avenue, Oneida, a city in Madison County, east of Wampsville, New York, so named for the Oneida tribe which had a large territory around Oneida Lake during the colonial period. She was one of five sisters and five brothers born to Joyce and Maurice Barcomb and attended Oneida High School. She graduated in 1977 with plans to move to California. Today, she is home in Oneida, buried in St Patrick's Cemetery alongside her parents. Her aunt Arlene remembers 'a bubbly little girl.' 'She was such a tiny little thing that couldn't have weighed more than 90 pounds,' Arelene told Jolene Cleaver of the New Haven Register in 2012.

Alcala struck again in December 1977, when he raped, sodomised and murdered Georgia Wixted, a 27-year-old cardiac care nurse at Centinela Hospital. He used a hammer to sexually abuse his victim and used the claw end to smash her head in. He then strangled her using a nylon stocking, before posing her naked body by her brass bed in her Malibu apartment. She was found, with a hammer next to her, on December 16. On June 24, 1978, Alcala raped, beat and murdered Charlotte Lamb, a legal secretary aged in her early 30s. He strangled her using a lace from her shoe, and left her body posed in the laundry room of an El Segundo apartment complex. She was found that same day by the apartment manager, lying face up with her hands behind her back. The residents of the complex had never seen her before.

That year, Alcala took an unusual step. The Dating Game was a popular TV show where single women chose a bachelor to go on a date with. The contestants were hidden from each other's view and had to rely on questioning only to make their choice. Occasionally, the roles were reversed, and single men got to choose a date. Other times, celebrities would take part, and future celebrities too. Before fame came their way, Farrah Fawcett, Lindsay Wagner, Tom Selleck, Steve Martin, Burt Reynolds, Arnold Schwarzenegger and Lee Majors appeared as contestants. As did a certain Rodney Alcala, a handsome fashion photographer. He didn't seem to be different to any other contestant—but if checks had been carried out, producers would have realised that he'd been convicted of raping an eight-year-old girl. And by the time he appeared on the show, he had got away with murder.

The episode was aired on September 13, 1978. Viewers had come to expect plenty of unsubtle and often uncomfortable innuendo. Host Jim Lange introduced Bachelor Number One as 'a successful photographer who got his start when his father found him in the darkroom at the age of 13, fully developed. Between takes you might find him skydiving or motorcycling. Please welcome Rodney Alcala.' When bachelorette Cheryl Bradshaw asked, 'I am serving you for dinner—what are you called, and what do you look like?', Bachelor Number One replied, 'I'm called the banana and I look really good… peel me.' Corny, unsubtle, provocative, outlandish—call it what you will, and the audience lapped it up. So did Cheryl, who picked Alcala.

Before filming, Alcala had unsettled one of the other contestants. 'He was a real creepy guy, a real idiot,' actor

Jed Mills, Bachelor Number Two, told Inside Edition. 'This creep comes up and he puts his face practically in my face, and he says, I always get the girl.' Cheryl had a similar experience when she met Alcala backstage afterwards. 'He was quiet, but at the same time he would interrupt and impose when he felt like it. He became very unlikable and rude and imposing as though he was trying to intimidate,' she told CNN in 2010. 'I wound up not only not liking this guy. He was a standout creepy guy in my life.' The pair never went on that date; Cheryl had a lucky escape.

Tragically, that was not the case for Jill Parenteau. Almost a year later, on June 14, 1979, the 21-year-old computer programme keypunch operator was raped and strangled to death. Her nude body was found on the bedroom floor, propped up by pillows. The culprit had broken into her Burbank apartment by jimmying the window louvres—and had cut themselves in the process. Alcala was later linked to the crime based on a semi-rare blood match. He was charged with murder, but the case was dismissed. That same year, on June 20, 12-year-old Robin Samsoe, from Huntingdon Beach, was happily playing on the beach with her best friend Bridget when a man approached the pair and asked if he could photograph them. When an adult checked in on the girls, the stranger fled the scene. Shortly afterwards, the two girls parted company and Robin headed to her ballet class on a borrowed bicycle. She never arrived. On July 2, her remains, scavenged by wild animals, was found 40 miles away, off Santa Anita Canyon Road near the Sierra Madre in the foothills of the San Gabriel Mountains. Her friend Bridget gave a description of the man who approached them at the beach, and the drawing was circulated to police stations. It was recognised by Alcala's parole officer and he was arrested.

In his cell, Alcala's sister paid him a visit. Officials listened to the conversation, during which Alcala asked his sister to clear out a locker he had in Seattle. On July 26, Huntingdon Beach detectives opened that same storage locker and discovered hundreds of graphic photographs of young women and girls, plus a bag containing items they suspected belonged to Alcala's victims. The haul included a pair of earrings, which were identified by Robin Samsoe's mother as the pair her daughter was wearing the day she disappeared. On May 8, 1980, Alcala was charged, tried and convicted for murdering Robin. He was sentenced to receive the death penalty but four years later the conviction was overturned by the California Supreme Court on a technicality; the appeal claimed that including previous convictions during the trial had prejudiced the jury. Alcala was retried and convicted again in 1986 but that, also, was overturned on another technicality by the 9th Circuit Court of Appeals. The judge had 'precluded the defence from developing and presenting evidence material to significant issues in the case.' During this time, more cold case files were reopened, and Alcala fought against having his DNA tested. He also wrote a book, called You The Jury, in which he protested his innocence.

In 2003, while preparing their third prosecution, Orange County investigators learned that Alcala's DNA, sampled under a new state law and over his objections, matched semen left at two crime scenes in Los Angeles. Another pair of earrings found in Alcala's storage locker matched the DNA of one of these two victims. Additional evidence, including another cold case DNA match in 2004, led to Alcala's indictment for the murders of Jill Barcomb (originally thought to have been a victim of the Hillside Strangler), Georgia Wixted, Charlotte Lamb and Jill Parenteau. Prosecutors also brought something new to the table: a pattern to the killing. They said Alcala played with his victims, almost killing them several times before raping them and finally strangling them. He also posed his victims in degrading positions and kept trophies.

A surprise witness at this third trial was Tali Shapiro, Alcala's first known victim. She told jurors how Alcala lured her into his car as she was walking home from school to the historic Chateau Marmont, where the family had only recently moved after their home had burned down. Alcala apologised to Shapiro in court, which understandably did not sit well with her. She said later: 'He's never apologised before, and for him to even bother, I mean, that made me sick to my stomach.' It was the only time he offered any remorse for his actions, and at a time in the trial when the jury was deciding whether to recommend a life sentence or the death penalty. Monique Hoyt was so disturbed at confronting Alcala in court that an LAPD detective sat next to her during her testimony. She told jurors how she managed to escape only by telling Alcala that she wanted a relationship with him.

Alcala represented himself at the trial. He did not contest that he murdered the four women in Los Angeles, preferring to focus on the charges against him relating to Robin Samsoe. He claimed that on the afternoon of her death, he was at Knott's Berry Farm, a theme park in Buena Park, California. Alcala called Robin's mother to the stand and tried to make her look bad to the jurors. She later described that face-to-face interaction with her daughter's killer as 'one of the hardest things I've ever had to do in my life.' Taking the stand himself, Alcala actually questioned himself in the third person for five hours, changing his tone depending on whether he was acting as himself or his lawyer. The only witness he called on to testify for him was psychiatrist Dr Richard Rappaport, who said Alcala suffered from borderline personality disorder, which may explain why he claimed he could not remember his violent attacks. The psychiatrist had agreed to testify after Alcala had asked him: 'Explain how you can commit crimes not in your memory.'

During closing arguments, Orange County Deputy District prosecutor Matt Murphy said Alcala was an 'evil monster who knows what he's doing is wrong and doesn't care.' While he had grown up with a loving mother who'd given her son every opportunity to succeed, including piano lessons and a private school education, he killed his victims for pleasure, like a psychopath. The photographs discovered in Alcala's possession were released, and Murphy added: 'We fear he is one of the most prolific serial killers on the West Coast in the 1970s, up there with Ted Bundy. He is a predatory monster, and when you see all these young women in positions of vulnerability with him, it makes you fear what happened to them.'

Alcala was now aged in his 60s. On February 25, 2010, after six weeks of testimony, he was found guilty of all five counts of capital murder, one count of kidnapping and four counts of rape. The jury took less than two days to reach their verdict. In a last-ditch attempt to avoid the death penalty, he played an 18-minute long Vietnam war protest song, Alice's Restaurant by Arlo Guthrie, which includes lyrics about killing.

He told the jurors that if they gave him the death penalty, 'you become a wannabe killer in the waiting'. A sentence of life in prison without parole 'would end this matter now.' he said. A most peculiar strategy, and one that had no effect—they recommended the death penalty anyway. Orange County Judge Francisco Briseno sentenced Alcala to death several weeks after the jury's recommendation. Briseno said Alcala had an abnormal interest in young girls. The photographs taken by him displayed 'sadistic sexual motives', and he reminded the court that some of his victims were posed after death.

In the same year of the trial, Seattle police named him as a person of interest in the unsolved murders of 13-year-old Antoinette Wittaker on July 1977, and 17-year-old Joyce

Gaunt in February 1978. Other cold cases were reportedly targeted for re-investigation in California, New York, New Hampshire and Arizona. In March 2011, investigators in Marin County, California, north of San Francisco, announced they were 'confident' that Alcala was responsible for the murder of 19-year-old Pamela Jean Lambson in 1977, who disappeared after making a trip to Fisherman's Wharf to meet a man who had offered to photograph her. Her battered, naked body was subsequently found in Marin County near a hiking trail. With no fingerprints or usable DNA, it was unlikely that charges could have been filed at the time. Now, police were claiming there was sufficient evidence to suggest Alcala committed the crime. In 2012, a Manhattan grand jury indicted Alcala for the murders of TWA flight attendant Cornelia Crilley and Ciro's heiress Ellen Hover. He was extradited to New York and initially denied both counts but pleaded guilty to two first-degree murders when he was told it was not guaranteed that he could have unlimited access to legal materials while under trial.

Cornelia Michel Crilley was found strangled in her apartment in 1971 during a time when Alcala was enrolled at NYU. With no leads, the case went cold for 39 years. In 2010, a fingerprint taken from the murder scene was matched positively to Alcala. In 1977, with the permission of his parole officer, Alcala had arranged to return to New York City—the same week 23-year-old Ellen Jane Hover went missing. Her disappearance became high profile very quickly, as she was Dean Martin and Sammy Davis Jr.'s goddaughter. Her father

Herman Hover had managed Ciro's, a nightclub popular with celebrities on the Sunset Strip. Ellen's decomposed body was found in 1978. With DNA technology sufficiently evolved, Alcala was linked to the murder. Police also knew he'd gone under an alias during that time: on Ellen's calendar on the day she vanished was a meeting with John Berger. On January 7, 2013, Alcala—who had already been sentenced to death in California—was sentenced to an additional 25 years to life in New York for the women's murders. The death penalty had not been an option in New York State since 2007 and Manhattan Criminal Court Judge Bonnie Wittner cried as she handed down the sentences down, commenting: 'This kind of case, I have never experienced, and I hope to never again.'

Detectives remain certain that final tally of murders committed by Rodney Alcala is incomplete. When the last trial had ended, Huntingdon Beach Police Department released 120 of Alcala's photographs, in the hope that some of the women could be identified. The collection included co-workers, classmates, girlfriends, family members and strangers. About 900 images were withheld because they were too graphic and disturbing to be shown to the public. None of the women were linked to missing person cases until 2013, when they were sent to Kathy Thornton by her son. As she sifted through the images, she came across her sister Christine, who had been missing since 1977. Christine had last been seen travelling across America with her boyfriend. Kathy had never given up trying to find her, and there she was, sitting astride a motorcycle, smiling at the camera. Kathy submitted her DNA for testing against a database of missing people in the hope of ending 30 years of uncertainty. It came back as a positive match to an unidentified body discovered in Sweetwater County, Wyoming in 1982. It transpired that Christine, then 28, spilt from her boyfriend and continued her journey alone when she met Alcala. At the time of her death, she was six months pregnant. Alcala admitted taking the photo but not to killing her. In September 2016, at the age of 73, Alcala was indicted for the murder and was reportedly 'too ill' to make the journey from California to Wyoming to stand trial.

Alcala remains in San Quentin maximum security correctional facility for men, near San Francisco, pending further appeals of his death sentences. The penitentiary is the state's oldest prison and was the only facility that conducted executions. It has a gas chamber, but since 1996, executions at the prison had been carried out by lethal injection. The prison has not performed an execution since 2006, when Clarence Ray Allen was put to death for three murders. Alcala is one of 737 inmates on death row, where state governor Gavin Newsom signed an order granting temporary reprieves to all condemned inmates. Meanwhile, detectives continue in their quest to identify the people Alcala photographed, wondering how many more fell victim to the handsome, charming, sadistic serial killer.

CHAPTER 8

DONALD NEILSON

THE BLACK PANTHER

*'I will get this callous killer if it is the last thing I
do.'—Detective Chief Superintendent Bob Booth.*

A MERICA HAS a superhero film called Black Panther,
based on the Marvel Comics character of the same
name. The French town of Armentieres, near Lille, had
its black panther when an animal of the genus name Panthera
was spotted perching on the ledge of a building and pacing
rooftops. Then there was Britain's Black Panther, who took on
an altogether different type of prowling as an armed robber,
kidnapper and murderer. Three men and a teenage girl's lives
were cruelly ended by a small, athletic, ferocious individual said
to be suffering from a severe psycho-pathological condition.

Donald Neilson was born Donald Nappey in Bradford on
August 1, 1936. His childhood was marred by his surname,

which he was teased and bullied at school for. He was also affected by the death of his mother from cancer when he was 11 years old. At 18, he entered statutory National Service in the King's Own Yorkshire Light Infantry. Like all British infantry regiments, it became a single-battalion unit in 1948 and served in Malaya during the Emergency (1948-1960) until 1951, when it joined the occupation forces in West Germany and West Berlin. In 1954 the battalion was sent to Kenya, and the following year to Aden before finding itself in Cyprus during the EOKA conflict.

In April 1955, with National Service behind, Neilson married his girlfriend, 20-year-old Irene Tate, at St Paul's Church, in Morley, near Leeds. In 1960 Irene, two years his senior, gave birth to their daughter Kathryn, and it was then that Neilson changed his surname by deed poll, principally because the teasing had continued during National Service and he didn't want his daughter to endure the same humiliation. Despite his enthusiasm for military life, Irene persuaded her husband against pursuing a full-time career in the Army. Instead, with the family settled in Bradford, he became a jobbing builder, but it did not go well, nor when he set up a taxi firm. By 1965, and short on cash, he turned his mind to burglary. He quickly became known to the West Yorkshire constabulary due to his technique of using a brace and bit to drill a hole in a window frame and then using a screwdriver or coat hanger to open the catch. Police dubbed the skilled burglar the Brace and Bit Robber. If the word successful applied to Neilson, then that is what he was—robbing countless homes without being caught. In 1967 his exploits took on a more ominous turn when he began to target sub-Post Offices, committing armed break-ins across Yorkshire, Lancashire and the West Midlands. With more than 23,000 such lightly defended offices dotted throughout the UK, Neilson must have viewed them as easy pickings. By 1974 he had targeted 18.

Heywood, a town in Lancashire, has an interesting history. For starters, it has the nickname Monkey Town, thought to originate from an area called Heap Bridge, or 'ape bridge' as local Irish immigrants pronounced it. With the nickname came the production of stools with holes in them, supposedly for a monkey's tail (in reality, to make them easy to carry). Peter Heywood, a member of the historic family and resident of Heywood Hall, was reputedly the man who snatched the torch from Guy Fawkes in the cellars of the Houses of Parliament, thereby preventing the success of the Gunpowder Plot. In 1789 a second Peter Heywood joined the mutineers aboard HMS Bounty. Fast forward to February 16, 1972, when Donald Neilson brought the small town back into the public eye after breaking into its sub-Post Office. Postmaster Leslie Richardson woke up and was wandering outside his bedroom when he came face to face with a figure wearing a dark-coloured balaclava. A struggle broke out and the intruder's shotgun went off, the bullet making a hole in the ceiling. The hooded figure escaped through the back door, but not before Richardson tore off the man's balaclava and got a good look at his face. The police put together what would prove to be the first of six photofit pictures of the intruder. Unfortunately, not one of them managed to resemble any of the others or, in fact, the actual perpetrator, Neilson.

Two years on, in 1974, Neilson selected a sub-Post Office in Harrogate, Yorkshire. Having gained entry, he tied up sub-postmaster Donald Skepper's 18-year-old son before confronting Skepper, who was in bed with his wife. When he tried to tackle the intruder, Skepper was fatally shot and Neilson fled the scene empty-handed. It was six months before he struck again, this time in the Higher Baxendale locale south of Accrington, Lancashire. Derek Astin was in bed with his wife when he was awoken by an intruder. A fight ensued and Astin was shot, who later died in hospital from his wounds. Again, Neilson evaded capture and it was at this time that he gained the nickname the Black Panther. During an interview with a local television reporter, Astin's wife Marion described the killer as 'so quick, he was like a panther.' The reporter, alluding to the culprit's dark clothing, ended his story by asking: 'Where is this Black Panther?'

Two months later, Sidney Grayland answered a knock at the back door of his sub-Post Office in Langley, West Midlands. He was confronted by a figure wearing a balaclava, wielding a torch and a bottle of ammonia. Unfortunately for Neilson, he somehow squirted himself and as a result ripped off his headwear. Grayland's wife appeared and Neilson attacked her, fracturing her skull. Grayland was shot dead in the scuffle before Neilson escaped with £800 in Postal

Orders from the safe. Afterwards, Mrs Grayland's description showed no great similarities to previous photofits but the police knew they were dealing with a lone attacker due to identical bullets being used.

In 1972, during his sub-Post Office spree of raids, Neilson read an article in the Daily Express about teenager Lesley Whittle, who had been left a large sum of money in the will of her deceased father, George, a prominent coach company owner. To avoid estate duties, George Whittle had given three houses plus £70,000 in cash to his girlfriend Dorothy, £107,000 to his son Ronald, and £82,500 to Lesley—and nothing to his estranged wife, Selina, who began legal proceedings in May 1972 to obtain money from her husband's estate. The story was picked up by the Express and, having read about the dispute and short of money himself, Neilson decided he was going to kidnap either Ronald or Dorothy for a £50,000 ransom. Police subsequently found out that Neilson had planned the crime for three years. On January 14, 1975, he drove to the Whittle's house in the close-knit former mining village of Highley, Shropshire, ready to execute it—taking 17-year-old A-level student Lesley instead. During the night, Neilson snatched the girl from her bedroom, allowing her to put on a blue candlewick dressing gown and slippers before placing a sticking plaster across her mouth and eyes. He taped her hands together, led her to his car and sped off. At about 7am, her mother Dorothy noticed Lesley's absence at breakfast. On the lounge table she found three ransom notes, punched out on a long strip of Dymo plastic tape, and left on a box of chocolates. The notes read:

> NO POLICE £50000 RANSOM TO BE READY TO
> DELIVER WAIT FOR TELEPHONE CALL AT SWAN
> SHOPPING CENTRE TELEPHONE BOX 6 PM TO 1
> PM IF NO CALL RETURN FOLLOWING EVENING
> WHEN YOU ANSWER GIVE NAME ONLY AND
> LISTEN YOU MUST FOLLOW INSTRUCTIONS
> WITHOUT ARGUMENT FROM TIME YOU ANSWER
> YOU ARE ON A TIME LIMIT IF POLICE OR
> TRICKS DEATH
> SWAN SHOPPING CENTRE KIDDERMINSTER
> DELIVER £50000 IN A WHITE VAN
> £50000 IN ALL OLD NOTES £25000 IN £1
> NOTES AND £25000 IN £5 THERE WILL BE NO
> EXCHANGE ONLY AFTER £50000 HAS BEEN
> CLEARED WILL VICTIM BE RELEASED

Frantic and fearing for their daughter's safety, the Whittles ignored Neilson's warnings to avoid contact with the police, and a surveillance operation was set up to catch him as the ransom was delivered. The investigation was led by Detective Chief Superintendent Bob Booth, the then head of West Mercia CID, a proud officer who had been awarded an MBE for solving the 70 murders that had landed on his desk. 'This man is a cold, cool, very calculating individual who is ruthless when cornered,' he said. 'This man is the most dangerous criminal at large in the country

today.' Booth and his colleagues were extremely conscious
that the steps taken in no way compromised the safety of
innocent lives. Murder Squad detectives were loaned from
Scotland Yard and led by Detective Chief Superintendent
John Morrison, who was duly despatched to the Midlands.

Two days after the abduction, the telephone rang in
the Whittle household. At the end of the line was Lesley,
who had been forced by her kidnapper to record a message.
'There is nothing to worry about mum. I am okay,' she said,
'I got a bit wet, but I am quite dry now and I am being
treated very well, okay?' The message lasted one minute and
29 seconds—and Lesley was definitely not okay. Neilson
had driven her 70 miles to Bathpool Park, situated in rural
Staffordshire near the border with Cheshire, not far from
Kidsgrove. The 178-acre public park is home to woodland
walks and bridle paths around a lake and several ponds,
where mature trees support a variety of wildlife. All that
was far from the Black Panther's mind as he shoved his
terrified victim down a drainage shaft linking to an underground labyrinth of drainage passageways, built decades
before. Lesley was left alone in her subterranean prison, in
the dark and on a narrow ledge with a wire noose strung
around her neck, secured with two clamps.

A freelance reporter got wind of the abduction and
reported it to a radio station which broadcast the news,
much to the annoyance of the police. They promptly withdrew Lesley's brother Ronald from an initial ransom plan
to avoid spooking the kidnapper into believing it was a

honeytrap. The following night, a hoax call at a telephone kiosk sent Ronald to a false rendezvous. That same night, angry that the ransom had not paid dividends, Neilson drove to Dudley, where he attempted to rob the Freightliner security depot. Security guard Gerald Smith was shot six times. Neilson left behind a stolen getaway car, a green Morris 1300, a few hundred yards from where Smith lay injured. It was another eight days before the police found and searched the vehicle, at which time they discovered a sleeping bag, torches, a gun and ammunition, some Dymo tape... and a tape recording of Lesley's voice.

Three days after Lesley was abducted, Ronald again picked up the ringing house telephone to hear a recording of his sister's voice, instructing him to wait at a telephone box in Kidsgrove. He headed to Bridgnorth police station, where he received a briefing from Detective Chief Superintendent Lovejoy, of Scotland Yard. Ronald then drove to Kidsgrove, with several unmarked police cars following his every move. Little did he realise how close he came to where Lesley was being held. He was running late and kept getting lost in the dark, it was 3am before he eventually arrived at the location specified by the kidnapper. Then it took another 30 minutes for him to find the next set of instructions, sending him to Bathpool Park. He was told to wait for the kidnapper to signal to him by flashing a torch. Coincidentally, a couple in a car was also at the spot and, puzzled by the flashing torchlight, caused confusion. In the end, Ronald gave up and went home.

By now, police had linked evidence in the abandoned stolen car in Dudley to the sub-Post Office murders, realising exactly who the kidnapper was and the chilling fact that they were dealing with a killer. By the beginning of March, the hunt switched back to Bathpool Park. A fortnight earlier, two schoolboys had stumbled upon the second ransom trail. There was a Dymo tape of instructions referring to the ransom cash being put down a hole, possibly relating to one of three manholes in the park. By March 7, a team of 50 officers was searching the park, and the authorities came to the tragic conclusion that they were no longer expecting Lesley to be found alive. 'The answer to the case lies here,' Chief Inspector Leonard Barnes told the Press, 'we have got to find it.' That same day, Lesley's body was discovered hanging from the bottom ledge of a sewer shaft, her feet mere inches from the ground. The wire around her neck had snagged on a stanchion and she had died of a fatal shock to the nervous system. Phil Maskery, the scenes of crime officer, was the first to venture into the drainage system and what he saw shocked the nation.

'I will get this callous killer if it is the last thing I do,' said Chief Superintendent Booth. 'I have said all along what an evil and terribly wicked man we are hunting. That he should do such a thing to a girl is terrible. We will get him, make no mistake about it.' How Lesley came to die so tragically remains a subject of conjecture. Whether she had fallen by accident or Neilson had pushed her in anger at not receiving the ransom, we will never know. The case turned into a murder inquiry, and the hunt intensified for the Black Panther, Britain's most wanted man.

It is December 11, 1975. PC Anthony White, aged 26, is on foot patrol and PC Stuart MacKenzie, 29, is in a panda car. On Stainforth Street, in Mansfield Woodhouse, Nottinghamshire, they rendezvous and are busy bringing their pocket notebooks up to speed when they spot a figure carrying a holdall and hurrying along Leeming Lane. They stop the man, who gives his name as John Moxton, of Chapel-en-le-Frith. He claims to be a lorry driver who's just finished work. He then produces a double-barrelled 12-bore sawn-off shotgun from his holdall and pushes it through the patrol car window. PC White is forced into the back of the Ford Escort and PC MacKenzie is instructed to drive at a normal speed towards Rainworth and Blidworth. As the car approaches The Ship in Southwell Road, Rainworth, PC White makes a grab for the barrel of the shotgun and at the same time grabs the man around the neck. Pushing the gun upwards, it goes off. The fight spills out on to the street, and with the assistance of two members of the public, the man—Neilson—is overpowered and handcuffed to railings by a fish and chip shop. Paul Cullen was 18 years old when he witnessed the incident. He gave an interview to Chad reporter Nick Frame 40 years later, explaining how he saw the car's brakes slam on and hearing a gunshot. As Neilson was handcuffed to the railings, Cullen noticed bullets strapped to his belt and knives poking out from inside his open jacket. 'There was also a big sawn-off shotgun lying in the middle of the road. An inspector picked it up with a white handkerchief,' he told the reporter.

Leading the Staffordshire Police manhunt following the Whittle murder was Detective Chief Superintendent Harold Wright. The sight of Lesley's naked lifeless body in the glare of his torch haunted him for years. Recounting the ordeal, he told Steve Bird in a report for the Daily Mail on December 24, 2011: 'This was really nasty. Very nerve racking. She was a 17-year-old girl hanging underground in absolute darkness. I just felt terribly sorry for her. She had been kept a prisoner down there, before being hanged. She would have occasionally heard trains going by overhead or seen rats with the torch she had been given. It was no place for a girl.' In 2015, then aged 95, he told The Sentinel's John Woodhouse about the night officers arrived in Nottinghamshire with an escort to return Neilson to Staffordshire for questioning. Everything was done by the book, he said. An infamous photograph of Neilson sporting a black eye was taken; he'd sustained it during the scuffle with the officers and members of the public as he was captured. During the police interview, Neilson was slow to answer, and responded to questions with comments such as, 'I have to think' or 'I don't know'. According to Wright: 'It wasn't a case of him being questioned for half-an-hour and coughing it up.'

Neilson was arraigned on nine charges, the first being the theft of a double-barrelled 12-bore shotgun and cartridges from Dewsbury, Yorkshire. Eight further charges followed: stealing guns and ammunition with intent to endanger life, four murder charges and one of attempting to murder a police officer. Despite Neilson's reluctance to talk, the evidence was heavily stacked against him. It was, in fact, overwhelming. A search of his house in Bradford turned up items linked to his murderous spree, including the same type of wire found around Lesley Whittle's neck, weaponry, his Black Panther hoods—and a model of a black panther. Neilson later insisted that he never intended to kill Lesley, alluding to the point that he'd left her with life-saving supplies. The coroner's findings revealed that despite the food Neilson claimed he had given her, she had not eaten for at least three days, possibly due to being terrified. The conclusion was that she may have died through the shock of falling off the ledge, causing her heart to stop beating. Neilson also claimed that he had never intended to kill any of the sub-postmasters.

As the case was being prepared for court, in March 1976, security guard Gerald Smith, who was shot by Neilson during a raid in Dudley the year before, died from his injuries and the after-effects of the incident. But Neilson could not be charged under UK law which, at the time (but now no longer the case), declared that a murder charge could not be brought in respect of a victim who died more than a year and a day after the incident which caused their death. It was a blow, but work continued and, as well as Neilson's nine-hour-long police statement about heiress Lesley Whittle and other shorter statements, magistrates were finally presented with 245 witness reports and details of 848 exhibits. Neilson's trial began at Oxford Crown Court on June 14, 1976, before Mr Justice Mars-Jones, and 20 seats usually reserved for the Press had to be vacated to accommodate evidence. This included a scale model of the drainage system at Bathpool Park where Lesley had been imprisoned.

During the trial, Neilson's defence lawyer, Gilbert Gray QC, contended that Lesley had accidentally fallen and hanged herself. He also said that Neilson fed her chicken soup, spaghetti and meatballs, and bought her fish and chips, chicken legs and Polo mints; claims the prosecution contested. Items found by police in the shaft and the subterranean canal running below it included a sleeping bag designed to prevent hypothermia, mattresses, survival blankets and bags, a bottle of brandy, six paperback books, a copy of The Times and two magazines, a small puzzle and two brightly coloured napkins. Remaining true to his obsession with the military, in the witness box Neilson affected a military demeanour, standing to attention whenever the judge entered. He never took his jacket off despite the heat and would refer to his 'master plan'. He was in the witness box for 19 hours in all, boasting of his pride in the kidnapping 'operation', and claiming his 'conscience was clear' over Lesley's death. Prosecuting, Philip Cox QC said the decision to murder Lesley Whittle was 'totally consistent with the cold, logical, military approach adopted by the accused.' In his closing speech for the defence, Mr Gray QC asked the jury whether they believed that a hangman's noose would be padded and lagged with 77.5-inches of Elastoplast to avoid chafing, or that a scaffold would be cushioned for comfort by a rubber mattress and sleeping bags. Pointing out that Lesley would not have died if the wire had not snagged on a stanchion because her feet were only six inches from the bottom of the shaft, he told the court: 'This is not something the defence has made up. Her height from the neck was four feet and there was a five feet length of ligature, giving an overall length of nine feet. The drop from the landing to the floor of the tunnel was six feet eleven inches, so that if it had not been for the unforeseen snagging which shortened the tether, there would have been two feet to spare and she would have landed on her feet at the bottom of the shaft.' He then asked the jury why Neilson had bothered to keep her alive once he'd recorded the ransom messages; he could have simply clubbed her to death and hidden the body in woodland. 'I submit that when Lesley Whittle went over the platform it was an unlooked-for misadventure, unplanned and undesired. Neilson started something that went hideously wrong.'

The jury was unconvinced, and on July 1, 1976, Neilson was unanimously convicted and given a life sentence for each of the four murders he was tried for. The jury had taken just two hours to reject Neilson's suggestion that Lesley Whittle had fallen to her death accidentally, and instead convicted him of executing his promise to kill her if the kidnap plot failed. The judge also gave Neilson a further 61 years: 21 years for kidnapping Lesley and 10 years for blackmailing her mother. Three further terms of 10 years each were imposed for the two burglary charges from which he stole guns and ammunition, and for possessing the sawn-off shotgun with intent to endanger life. All the sentences were to run concurrently. Neilson was found not guilty of the attempted murders of sub-postmistress Margaret Grayland and PC Tony White, who was injured in the hand when the firearm went off in the panda car, but guilty of the lesser alternative charges of inflicting grievous bodily harm on Mrs Grayland and of possessing a shotgun with the intent of endangering life at Mansfield. The shooting of security guard Gerald Smith was ordered to lie on file due to the legal complications involved.

The public watching from the gallery cheered as guilty verdicts rang around the courtroom, and Dorothy Whittle hugged her son. Neilson remained impassive in the dock as Mr Justice Mars-Jones told him that the enormity of his crimes put him in a class apart from almost all convicted murderers, and that he should never taste freedom again. The judge sympathised with the jury over the amount of evidence they were forced to hear before reaching their verdict, and he later recommended to the Home Office that each of the jurors should be declared exempt from jury service for the following 10 years. Neilson's defence team—the solicitor Barrington Black, junior counsel Norman Jones and leading counsel Gilbert Gray—claimed his conviction was simply a reflection of public opinion and a backlash from the publicity given to the search for Lesley, and that he should have been convicted only of the lesser charge of manslaughter. After the verdicts were delivered, Mr Gray visited his client in a cell below the courthouse. He found Neilson curled up in the foetal position in a corner, dejected and allegedly filled with remorse for Whittle and her family. Mr Black later described his client as 'evil and one of the most notorious criminals of the decade.' After his conviction, Neilson spent much of his time in jail at Full Sutton Prison, near York. He only ever appealed against one conviction, that of the murder of Lesley Whittle. It was rejected in 1977.

Later, Neilson's wife Irene was charged and convicted of seven offences of handling stolen postal orders—postal orders her husband stole from the post offices he raided, and which she claimed she had been forced to cash. Her solicitor, Barrington Black, placed the blame squarely on Neilson's complete domination of his wife, describing him as a 'Svengali who had exercised a hypnotic influence. He was a quasi-military figure who barked orders at his wife and daughter, and woe betide anyone who disobeyed him.' He told the court that at home Neilson 'became a strict disciplinarian… who barked like a sergeant major and told his wife and daughter what to do.' The defence team anticipated probation, but magistrates jailed Irene Whittle for 12 months, stating that while they had every sympathy with a lady before the courts for the first time, they regarded her activities as a deliberate course of conduct. An appeal was immediately lodged, at which Donald Neilson told the court: 'I was the boss at home and there was no doubt about it... what I said went and if this involved knocking about, it had to be.'

Criminologist Terry Hayden said Neilson was 'uninteresting' compared to other serial killers. 'He did not captivate the public imagination,' he commented. 'This was the 1970s when we had Myra Hindley and Ian Brady. You look at someone like Dennis Neilson and there was more in the psychology of it, more for people to get their teeth into. People are more interested in the more gruesome ones. This guy was just evil. He was not particularly calculating. There was not an intent to catch and kill, it was a means to commit robbery.'

In 2008, Neilson applied to the High Court to have his minimum term reverted to 30 years. On June 12, his appeal was rejected, and he was told by Mr Justice Teare that he would spend the rest of his life in prison: 'This is a case where the gravity of the applicant's offences justifies a whole life order. The manner in which the young girl was killed demonstrates that it involved a substantial degree of premeditation or planning. It also involved the abduction of the young girl. The location and manner of Lesley Whittle's death indicates that she must have been subjected by the applicant to a dreadful and horrific ordeal.' In 2009 it was revealed that Neilson had been diagnosed with the irreversible muscle-wasting condition motor neurone disease and was transferred from HMP Full Sutton to Norwich Prison. In the early hours of December 18, 2011, the Black Panther, then aged 75, was taken from jail to Norfolk and Norwich

University Hospital suffering from a chest infection and pneumonia. The man described at his trial as 'a frustrated military man of modest rank, a Lance Corporal who fancied himself as a general' was pronounced dead the next day.

The inquest heard that Neilson had asked prison staff to not keep him alive if his health deteriorated. Coroner William Armstrong said Neilson's family had been informed of the hearing but had taken the decision to stay away. According to a report on The Independent's website by Ben Kendall on August 9, 2012, relatives did not visit Neilson while he was in jail, although his daughter Kathryn did send prison staff a card thanking them for the care they provided. 'At the time of his death he struggled to do even the most basic things and was virtually dependent on other people,' said Mr. Armstrong. Claire Watson, offender health commissioner for Norfolk and Waveney NHS, told the inquest that at the time of his transfer in April 2009, Neilson had become increasingly dependent on others, and that Norwich Prison was thought to be the best place for his needs. 'Prisons aren't the best place for people who can't dress themselves and can't wash themselves,' she said. Having overseen a review of Neilson's care, she said he was a challenging and uncooperative patient, and prison staff should be commended for their care, which was equitable with that he would have received in the community. A jury returned a verdict that Neilson died of natural causes.

Like many killers, Neilson's life and crimes were portrayed in film. The Black Panther, starring Donald Sumpter in the title role, was released in 1977 and made available on DVD in 2012. A fictionalised account of the Whittle kidnapping and Neilson's trial formed the basis of Adam Mars-Jones's short story, Bathpool Park. His father, Sir William Mars-Jones, had presided over the trial and Adam had served as his marshal.

When Neilson was captured, he boasted about the people he killed: how he'd shot dead three sub-postmasters in the space of nine months during violent robberies. The former Lance Corporal who had so enjoyed the macho military lifestyle and playing at soldiers prided himself on being responsible for more than 400 burglaries, all committed in his trademark black clothes. The authorities had earmarked him as a ruthless criminal, and he no doubt enjoyed the attention he received in the media as the Black Panther. In reality, he was a wily 5ft 6in tall nobody who grabbed the country's attention due to his audacity and cunning. In the end, he was simply another cold-blooded, vicious, controlling killer; a narcissist and a pathetic little man who had shot innocent people and kept his kidnapping victim tethered like a dog. He showed no remorse for his horrific deeds and died a sad, lonely death, ravaged by a disease from which there was no escape. Inside the porch of St Mary's Church in the village of Highley, Ronald Whittle and his mother Dorothy had a small brass plaque mounted to mark their loss. It reads: In loving memory George Whittle (1905-1970) and his daughter Lesley Whittle (1957-1975).

CHAPTER 9

PETER SUTCLIFFE

THE YORKSHIRE RIPPER

*'Killing prostitutes had become an obsession
with me and I couldn't stop myself. It was like
some sort of a drug.'—Peter Sutcliffe.*

MENTION THE name Peter William Coonan in a pub quiz and many people will be perplexed. Then mention Peter William Sutcliffe, and the name needs little introduction. In 1981, Sutcliffe, known as The Yorkshire Ripper, was convicted of murdering 13 women and attempting to murder seven others.

Bingley is located on the edge of the Yorkshire Dales, just down the Aire Valley from the attractive Brontë area, a region rich in history with the prehistoric Rombalds Way approaching from the east, passing across Ilkley Moor and on to the west coast. There is much in the way of recent history, with the mills, railway and the Leeds Liverpool canal springing from the Industrial Revolution. Peter Sutcliffe was born prematurely in this small provincial town on June 2, 1946, to a working-class family. His parents, John William and Kathleen Frances (née Coonan) ran a highly religious Catholic household. Young Peter, the oldest of six children, had a fond relationship with his mother but he was afraid of his alcoholic father. With few friends to speak of, he was bullied at school and left at the age of 15, taking a succession of odd jobs. The one he most identified with was digging graves at Bingley Cemetery, and such was his passion for the role that he often worked additional hours. He relished telling his small circle of friends that he had the best job in the world, and how much he enjoyed the sight of the corpses. Some analysts argue that the position gave him a fascination with death and the macabre elements of life, while others say it may have made him feel more isolated than he already was.

Sutcliffe was 21 years old when he met his future wife, Sonia Szurma, at a disco at a local public house on Valentine's Day, 1967. He and Sonia, who was born in 1951 to Czechoslovakian parents, tied the knot on August 10, 1974. She was studying to be a teacher when she was diagnosed with schizophrenia. Sonia also suffered several miscarriages over the following few years, and the couple were subsequently informed that she was unable to bear children. Two years after their wedding, his first offence involving a sex worker was recorded against Sutcliffe. He was a regular visitor to the red-light district of Bradford, and was driving with a friend when he got out of the car, chased and assaulted an alleged prostitute. He returned to the car, breathless, and told his friend he'd followed the woman to a garage, where he'd hit her on the head with a stone. When the authorities caught up with Sutcliffe the following day, no charges were brought.

Sutcliffe had always thought of his mother as the perfect woman. In 1970, his father accused his wife of cheating, and insulted her in front of the family. The incident had a profound impact on him, and possibly triggered in his mind the thought that all women were cheaters. Between November 1971 and April 1973, Sutcliffe worked at the Baird Television factory on a packaging line. By 1974 the industry was experiencing a dramatic fall in demand for consumer electronic goods, especially colour televisions. At the time, the UK was producing 2.5-million colour TV sets per annum, but then demand dropped to about 1.5-million, and forecasts were not favourable. Whether that had any impact on Sutcliffe's next decision is unknown, but after having demonstrated a modicum of prowess and good nature on the packaging line, he was offered a job as a travelling salesman, which he turned down. Instead he took up a position as a nightshift factory worker at the Britannia Works of Anderton International on Ferncliffe Road, Bingley. In February 1975, he took redundancy and used half of his pay-off to gain a licence as an HGV driver. He passed the test at Steeton driving school on June 4, 1975, two days after his 29th birthday. With his new licence in his pocket, on September 29 Sutcliffe gained employment as a driver for Common Road Tyre Services at Okenshaw. The work consisted of short and medium distance hauls across the north of the country and the Midlands, and soon Sutcliffe gained awareness and understanding of Britain's infrastructure, its trunk roads and motorways.

On October 30 that year, 28-year-old mother of four Wilma McCann was struck with a hammer and stabbed 15 times in the neck and chest—the first of 13 women murdered by Sutcliffe over the course of the next six years, a spree that sparked one of the biggest police manhunts in British history. The previous evening at about 7.30pm, McCann left her oldest child, a nine-year-old, in charge of their three siblings at home in Scott Hall Avenue, in the Chapeltown area of Leeds. She called in at various pubs before ending the evening at a drinking club called Room At The Top, leaving shortly before 1am. Worse for drink, she tried to flag down a passing motorist to drop her off at home, a short walk away. Sutcliffe happened to be in the vicinity in his lime green Ford Capri GT and saw McCann thumbing a lift. He picked her up and stopped near the Prince Phillip Playing Fields, about 100 yards from McCann's house, with the intention of having sex. Sutcliffe got out of the car and lay down his coat on the grass, concealing a hammer in his hand. When McCann sat down, Sutcliffe pounced. Her body was found at 7.41am the following morning by milkman Alan Routledge and his 10-year-old brother Paul. She was on her back, with her trousers down to her knees and her breasts exposed. She had suffered multiple stab wounds in her lower abdomen, chest and neck.

In his confession over the course of January 4 and 5, 1981, Sutcliffe would later state: 'That was the incident that started it all off. I was driving through Leeds late at night, I'd been to somewhere having a couple of pints, you'll know the date better than me. It was Wilma McCann. I was in a Ford Capri, K registered, a lime green one with a black roof with a sun grill in the back window. I saw this woman thumbing a lift where the Wetherby Road branches to the right, but you can carry straight on. She was wearing some white trousers and a jacket. I stopped and asked her how far she was going. She said not far, thanks for stopping, and she jumped in.' He explained how when they stopped, he took a hammer from his toolbox on the back seat of his car and hid it under a coat hanging over his arm. McCann sat down, he said, and unfastened her trousers, telling him to get on with it. 'Don't worry, I will,' he replied, before striking her on the head. Sutcliffe ran back to the car, expecting McCann to get up. When she didn't and, realising he would be in serious trouble if she told anyone, he took a knife from his toolbox and returned to her prone body. In a blind panic, he stabbed her repeatedly. 'What a damn stupid thing to do just to keep somebody quiet,' he said in his statement. 'If I was thinking logical at the time, I would have stopped and told someone I'd hit her with the hammer. That was the turning point. I realise I over-reacted at the time. Nothing I have done since then affected me like this.' At the time of the murder Sutcliffe was residing at his mother-in-law's, 44 Tanton Crescent, Clayton, Bradford. He checked his clothes for evidence, went to the bathroom to wash his hands and went to bed. The next day he watched a report of the murder on television. 'I felt sick and I still half expected a knock on the door by the police,' he said. 'I carried on trying to act as normal, living with my wife and in-laws. After that first time, I developed and built up a hatred for prostitutes in order to justify within myself the reason why I had attacked and killed Wilma McCann.'

In January 1976, Sutcliffe claimed his second victim. Emily Jackson was 42 and lived with her husband Sydney in Churwell, a suburb of Leeds located between the city centre and Morley. Her husband was a roofing contractor and did not drive, so Emily took him from job to job. To help ease financial pressures on the household, she also cruised the streets of Chapeltown, working as a part-time prostitute. The Jacksons enjoyed going to the Gaiety pub on Roundhay Road, Leeds. On the night of January 20, she left her husband in the bar while she stepped outside. Sutcliffe spotted her and she got into his car, driving to a piece of derelict land off the main road. He made an excuse that the car would not start, so they got out and as Emily's back was turned, Sutcliffe struck her twice with a hammer. He then stabbed her more than 50 times in the neck, breasts, lower abdomen and back with a Phillips screwdriver. Dumping her crumpled body in a yard, he returned to home. When Sydney left the pub a few hours later, he saw their van in the car park, but his wife was nowhere to be found, so he got a taxi home. Emily's body was spotted the following morning between two derelict buildings by a workman taking a short-cut through a passage between Manor Street and Roundhay Road. Police found her handbag nearby and noted a boot impression on her right thigh. Her dreadful injuries led officers to connect her murder with that of Wilma McCann. Sutcliffe later confessed that he'd driven to Leeds with an inner compulsion to kill a sex worker. He smelt her cheap perfume as she got into his car and felt compelled to 'get rid of her'.

On March 5, 1976, having become familiar with local routes around Yorkshire on his delivery rounds, Sutcliffe was dismissed by Common Road Tyre Services for stealing tyres. He was out of work for six months before securing a job as a HGV driver with T & W H Clark (Holdings) Ltd on Bradford's Canal Road Industrial Estate. Fast forward to September 1977, and Sutcliffe and his wife bought number 6 Garden Lane, in Heaton. By that time, he had claimed three more victims. Irene Richardson was 28 years old. Down on her luck, she took a room in a house on Cowper Street, Leeds. She was picked up by Sutcliffe, who drove her to Soldiers Field, where she got out of the car and crouched down to urinate on the grass. Sutcliffe struck her from behind with a hammer, before lifting her clothes and repeatedly stabbing her with a Stanley knife in the lower abdomen and slashing her throat. He covered her body with her imitation suede fur-trimmed coat before driving back home to Heaton. A jogger discovered Irene's body the following morning, and it proved to be a major breakthrough for the squad tasked with finding the killer. Tyre marks had been left on the soft ground of Soldiers Field: two India Autoway tyres, a cross-ply Pleumant and a cross-ply Esso 110. Investigators determined that with the rear track width to hand, the number of marques that this could apply to was 26, including the Ford Corsair—the exact car Sutcliffe was driving that night. It was going to prove a long haul for the murder squad, however, with 100,000 vehicles across West Yorkshire to check. That was if the killer had decided not to change his tyres in the meantime.

April 23, 1977. A Saturday. Thelma Houston was on the radio singing Don't Leave Me This Way and Abba was charting with Knowing Me, Knowing You. People were playing Air-Sea Battle and Depthcharge video games, and cinemagoers were watching films including The Man Who Loved Women, directed by Francois Truffaut. And the man who hated sex workers was on the prowl for his next victim. He picked up Patricia 'Tina' Atkinson, a 32-year-old from Bradford, on St Paul's Road and they drove to her flat in Oak Avenue, where she told Sutcliffe she lived alone. As he alighted the car, he picked up a claw hammer he'd purchased at Clayton hardware shop. Once inside the flat, and with her back towards him as she sat on the bed, Sutcliffe struck the back of her head with the hammer and she crumpled to the floor. He hit her several more times, placing her body on the bed and covering her with bedclothes. He then drove home and parked up in the garage, returning to normality.

His next victim was just 16. With the urge welling inside him to kill, Sutcliffe drove to Leeds in his Corsair and spotted shop assistant Jayne MacDonald walking along Chapeltown Road in the direction of Reginald Street and her home in Scott Hall Avenue—six doors away from the home of Wilma McCann, Sutcliffe's first murder victim. Believing her to be a prostitute, he parked his car at the Hayfield pub and backtracked to follow her. He struck her from behind with a hammer and dragged her body into a yard before hitting her again and driving home. Jayne's body was discovered near a wall at 9.45am by two children as they headed for an adventure playground between Reginald Street and Reginald Terrace. She had been struck three times on the head and stabbed multiple times. The public outcry at the young girl's death prompted Chief Constable Ronald Gregory to appoint his most senior detective, Assistant Chief Constable George Oldfield, to take overall charge of the murder investigations. Later, Sutcliffe told police: 'I read recently about her father dying of a broken heart and it brought it all back to me. I realised what sort of a monster I had become.' Former railwayman Wilf MacDonald passed away two years after his daughter's murder, never having recovered from the tragedy.

Sutcliffe's next attack was on Maureen Long. He spotted her walking along Manningham Lane towards the city centre. He pulled up and after a brief conversation she got into the car with him. They stopped at an area of land near where she lived, and Sutcliffe attacked her with a hammer and stabbed her several times in the chest and back. Believing her to be dead, he drove off. The next morning, he was shocked to learn through media reports that she'd survived, and even though he was concerned that she would be able to identify him, the impulse to hunt down and murder prostitutes was growing stronger. His last murder victim of 1977 was 20-year-old sex worker Jean Jordan in Manchester, the first of his targets beyond West Yorkshire. Sutcliffe picked her up on October 1, and her body was found on a disused allotment in Chorlton-cum-Hardy nine days later. She had suffered hammer blows to the head and had been savagely attacked with a knife. Having driven halfway home after the attack, Sutcliffe suddenly remembered he'd given Jean £5 for sex, a brand-new note he'd received in his pay packet from Clarks. With no mention of the murder on news bulletins over the following days, Sutcliffe returned to the body to search for the note. Jean was exactly where he had left her. Unable to find the note, in his frustration he slammed a pane of glass on her lifeless torso before attempting to sever her head with a blade.

Following the discovery of Jean's body, on October 15 investigators found her handbag containing the note. Assuming the money had been for services rendered, Chief Superintendent Ridgway, of the Greater Manchester Police, promptly linked the murder with the crimes in neighbouring West Yorkshire. Further investigation revealed that the note was probably from a consignment of five thousand delivered to the Manningham, Shipley and Bingley branches of the Midland Bank three days prior to the murder. Detectives from Greater Manchester and West Yorkshire joined forces to trace the note's owner, an inquiry which ran into the new year. Sutcliffe was interviewed by officers but not investigated any further—and that very same month, he killed again.

On January 21, 1978, Sutcliffe picked up 21-year-old Yvonne Pearson on Lumb Lane, Bradford. He later told how he drove along White Abbey Road and was directed by Pearson to turn left into a street by Silvios Bakery. He drove to the end of the street and parked up. Outside, he struck Yvonne twice on the head from behind with a hammer. He dragged her to some wasteland and was disturbed by an approaching car, which parked near his own. He hid behind an old sofa, and to stop Yvonne from moaning he shoved some of the sofa's horsehair filling into her mouth. Once the other car left, he placed the sofa over Yvonne's lifeless body and went home. She had been due to appear in court five days later on a charge of soliciting.

Before Yvonne's body was discovered, Sutcliffe targeted 18-year-old Helen Rytka in Huddersfield, on January 31. A few days earlier he'd driven there on a work delivery and had noticed prostitutes plying their trade. He returned to the red-light area and came across Helen with her sister. The siblings shared a house together. He drove her to the back of a timber yard between a stack of wood, where he attacked her with a hammer, and stopped when he saw two taxi drivers nearby. After they left, he stabbed Helen repeatedly and had sex with her limp body. He then covered her with an asbestos sheet. He struck again on May 16, this time attacking 40-year-old Vera Millward using a similar modus operandi: striking her from behind with a hammer when she was outside the back door of his car, about to climb into the back seat. He stabbed her before leaving her body where it was and driving off.

Eleven months later, on April 4, 1979, Sutcliffe happened upon 19-year-old Josephine Whitaker. He'd been driving around in his black fastback Sunbeam Rapier with no particular destination in mind and ended up in Halifax. He spotted Whitaker, parked his car and followed her before approaching her and starting a casual conversation. She told him she was returning home from her grandmother's house. As they were crossing a grass clearing, Sutcliffe hung back before striking her twice with a hammer. He then stabbed her repeatedly with a screwdriver, which he had been carrying in his pocket. Investigating the scene of the murder the following day, police noted a boot mark consistent with those found at the spots where Emily Jackson and Patricia Atkinson were found. They also came across traces of milling oil used in engineering shops, leading investigators to suppose that the culprit could be a lorry driver.

Barbara Leach was in her final year at university studying social psychology. On the evening of September 2, 1979, she was in the Mannville Arms, Bradford. Having left her friends, she decided to walk home alone, and Sutcliffe spotted her as she set off. He drove by before parking up a short distance away. As she walked past Sutcliffe's car, he attacked her from behind with a hammer and stabbed her with a screwdriver, leaving her body by some dustbins at the back of a property. Sutcliffe drove home and later disposed of the screwdriver over an embankment on the westbound side of Hartshead Service Station. It was the same instrument he'd used on Josephine Whitaker.

In 1980, Sutcliffe was interviewed by the police regarding the footprint found at the scene of Josephine's murder. Despite forensic evidence, he was allowed to leave because the attention of officers was diverted to a taped message from a man claiming to be the Yorkshire Ripper. Based on the accent, the man was believed to be from Wearside, an area of Sunderland. It turned out to be a hoax—in 2005, unemployed alcoholic John Samuel Humble was charged with perverting the course of justice. So, Sutcliffe went on to kill again. On August 20, 1980, 47-year-old Marguerite Walls was bludgeoned to death with a hammer in Leeds. On this occasion, Sutcliffe was without a knife so instead he strangled his victim with a length of cord. On Monday, November 17, Sutcliffe killed his 13th and final victim. Jacqueline Hill was 20 years old and in her third year of an English degree. Sutcliffe drove to Headingley, where he bought food from a Kentucky Fried Chicken restaurant. He then drove along Otley Road and spotted Hill walking towards Alma Road. He parked up and waited for her to pass, attacking her from behind with a hammer. He dragged her into an entrance to some wasteland and repeatedly stabbed her.

It was on Friday, January 2, 1981 that Sutcliffe made his mistake. He left home in Heaton and drove to a scrapyard where he salvaged two number plates. Although nothing is documented, it would be fair to assume that he fixed one of these to his car. He stopped prostitute Denise Hall, who was disturbed by him and told him she was unavailable. He then spotted Olivia Reivers who told him the price for sex was £10 if he used protection. Olivia got into the car and they drove for about half-a-mile before pulling over. A short time later, PC Robert Hydes drove by and ran a plate check on Sutcliffe's parked vehicle. The plates were for a different vehicle, so PC Hydes had a word. Sutcliffe said he needed the toilet and while pretending to urinate in nearby bushes, he disposed of the incriminating hammer and knife. At Dewsbury Police Station, Sutcliffe again asked to use the toilet, where he disposed of a knife in a cistern. The following day, the area where Sutcliffe had been with Denise Hall was searched and a hammer, knife and length of cord were found. The Yorkshire Ripper team was contacted and their interest in Sutcliffe intensified, particularly when they realised how many times he had already been interviewed in relation to the case. Every time he'd been ruled out because his accent did not match that of the hoax caller. After two days under interrogation, Sutcliffe confessed.

He was charged on January 5, 1981 and pleaded not guilty to 13 counts of murder but guilty to manslaughter on the grounds of diminished responsibility. The basis of his defence was that he claimed to be the tool of God's will; that he had heard voices ordering him to kill prostitutes while working as a gravedigger. Sutcliffe also pleaded guilty to seven charges of attempted murder. It had been the intention of the prosecution to accept his plea after four psychiatrists diagnosed him with paranoid schizophrenia. However, trial judge Justice Sir Leslie Boreham demanded a detailed explanation of the prosecution's reasoning before rejecting the plea and the expert testimonies of the psychiatrists, insisting that a jury should deal with the case. The trial commenced on May 5 and lasted two weeks. Sutcliffe was found guilty of murder on all counts and sentenced to 20 concurrent life sentences. Justice Boreham said Sutcliffe was beyond redemption and hoped he would never leave prison. He recommended a minimum term of 30 years to be served before parole could be considered. After his conviction, Sutcliffe began to use his mother's maiden name, and was known as Peter William Coonan.

More than 150 police officers had at one time or another been involved in the search for Sutcliffe. He was interviewed on nine separate occasions and despite witness descriptions and other circumstantial evidence tying him to the murders, there had never been enough evidence to physically arrest him. He began serving his sentence at HMP Parkhurst on May 22, 1981. On January 10, 1983, while in the hospital wing, he was seriously assaulted by a fellow prisoner who had several convictions for violence. The inmate twice plunged a broken coffee jar into the left side of Sutcliffe's face. He suffered four wounds, requiring 30 stitches. In March 1984

Sutcliffe was diagnosed with paranoid schizophrenia and transferred from prison to Broadmoor Hospital under Section 47 of the Mental Health Act 1983. In August 2016 he was ruled as mentally fit to be returned to prison and was transferred to HM Prison Frankland in Country Durham. In 2010, Sutcliffe launched a High Court bid to find out if he could one day be freed, after doctors at Broadmoor told his lawyers he was no longer dangerous. Lawyers acting on his behalf attempted to establish a minimum tariff, which could have one day seen him released on parole. Jack Straw, the then Justice Secretary, quashed his bid, saying there were 'no circumstances' in which he would be released. Former Prime Minister Gordon Brown also said it would be 'very unlikely' that Sutcliffe would be released, an assessment which was upheld in the High Court when it rejected the appeal, confirming that Sutcliffe would serve a whole life tariff and would never be released. In November 2017, Sutcliffe, aged 71, was admitted to hospital complaining of chest pains and shortness of breath. Once thoroughly checked over he was returned to his cell.

Sonia Sutcliffe had divorced her husband in 1994 and remarried three years later. Following Sutcliffe's conviction, she was constantly hounded by the Press and won almost a dozen libel cases, including one in 1989 against Private Eye. She sued the satirical news magazine after it detailed her attempts to make financial deals with newspapers and claimed she was attempting to profit from her husband's crimes. In court, George Carman, the magazine's QC, described her as 'dancing on the graves of her husband's victims'. She was awarded record libel damages of £600,000—£100,000 more than any previous award. The then editor Ian Hislop stated that 'if that's justice, I'm a banana', and announced an immediate intention to appeal. A crowd-sourced fund named Bananaballs was set up to pay for the appeal's legal costs, and the amount was eventually reduced to £60,000.

Meanwhile, West Yorkshire Police came under fire for being inadequately prepared for what transpired as one of the largest investigations by a British police force. Pre-dating the use of computers, and with information on suspects stored on handwritten index cards, officers found it difficult to overcome the information overload. Cross-referencing was difficult and was compounded by television appeals for information, which in turn generated thousands more documents. The Inspector of Constabulary Sir Lawrence Byford's report of an official inquiry into the Ripper case was not released by the Home Office until June 1, 2006, when it concluded that 'the ineffectiveness of the major incident room was a serious handicap to the Ripper investigation. While it should have been the effective nerve centre of the whole police operation, the backlog of unprocessed information resulted in the failure to connect vital pieces of related information. This serious fault in the central index system allowed Peter Sutcliffe to continually slip through the net.' In 2009, Channel 4 aired the Red Riding mini-series crime drama, which dealt with corruption in the Yorkshire police force and included the Yorkshire Ripper case as a backdrop. In March 2019 a three-part series, The Yorkshire Ripper Files: A Very British Crime Story by film-maker Liza Williams, aired on BBC Four, and included interviews with some of the victims, their families, police and journalists who covered the case.

Sutcliffe was interviewed no fewer than nine times in connection with the killings and released each time. As journalist Ed Power noted on the Daily Telegraph website: 'It was inevitable that the true crime craze would alight upon the Yorkshire Ripper and the bungled police hunt for the most notorious serial killer in modern British history. Thankfully, episode one of Liza Williams's three-part investigation into the case… resisted the temptation to fetishise Peter Sutcliffe. Williams instead told the story of the victims and how the misogyny of the era allowed the Ripper to stay at large long after he should have been apprehended.'

CHAPTER 10

PEDRO ALONSO LÓPEZ

MONSTER OF THE ANDES

*'I am the man of the century. No one will
ever forget me.'—Pedro López.*

OR A serial killer responsible for the murders of
more than 350 children, there is little wonder that
Pedro Alonso López was nicknamed the Monster of
the Andes. It was a moniker never to be forgotten, particularly as despite having admitted his crimes, in 1998 López
was set free, even though he had vowed to kill again. To
this day, no one knows of his whereabouts or whether he
ever murdered again.

López was born on October 8, 1948, in the shadow of
Santa Isabel, a shield volcano located in Tolima, one of the
32 departments of Colombia in the Andean region, in the
centre-west of the country. Today it is a magnet for serious

hikers, drawn by the 15,600ft snow-capped volcano set in the paralysing cold and stark beauty of the Alpine wilderness in the Nevados National Park. In 1948, Colombia was in the grip of widespread and systematic political violence, known as La Violencia. A 10-year civil war raged from 1948, fought mainly in the countryside. This intense political feud between Liberals and Conservatives had little to do with class conflict, foreign ideologies or other matters outside the Republic. It is estimated that more than 200,000 people lost their lives between 1946 and 1964 as a result. The most spectacular aspect of the violence, however, was the extreme cruelty perpetrated on the victims, a topic of continuing study for Colombians.

Midardo Reyes, a member of the Colombian Conservative Party during the civil war, had a fight with his wife one December night in 1947 and stormed out into the darkness. He ended up spending the evening with Belinda López de Castañeda, with whom reportedly he was having an affair. She was soon to discover that she was pregnant with Reyes's child, the seventh of 13 children born to her. Three months later, on April 9, 1948, Reyes was shot and killed by a rebellious mob while defending a grocery store where he happened to be. Six months later, his son, Pedro Alonso, was born in Santa Isabel. While his mother claimed to be loving and caring, López would later state that she was a prostitute and that she was cruel to him. From a young age he would watch her have sex with clients, and she would let them hit her on occasion. In a recorded interview, López claimed she was abusive: 'That woman was violent. It is my understanding that this woman is sick in the head because that was not the proper way to punish your children. She would punish me with such violence.' His mother, however, claimed that even though they were poor, she was loving. Her son, she said, was a bright child, and would help other children practice their vowels. He once said to her: 'Mum, isn't it true that I am good at teaching the children? One day I am going to be a teacher.'

There are conflicting reports of why López left the family home at eight years of age. One account states his mother caught him fondling his younger sister and so she evicted him. And yet, in a documentary, she said that when he ran away, she believed a neighbour had kidnapped him: 'That night I cried and cried. I looked all over for him, and I couldn't find him. Then I went to a man who was a fortune-teller and he said Pedro went in a car with a man. They killed his father and now my son was stolen.' Like so many other disowned children on the often-violent Colombian streets, López became a beggar. It was not long before he was approached by a man who sympathised with the boy's situation and offered him refuge and food on the table. Taking the man at his word, López tagged along but soon found himself in an abandoned building where he was repeatedly sodomised by the paedophile before being dumped back on the streets. Those acts of violence and abuse were to have a profound effect on the young López, who from that day forward vowed that he would do the same to as many little girls as he could. Mentally scarred by the incident, he joined a gang of street children for protection, and violence and hatred became his way of life. The gang often fought others with knives and belts for places to sleep in. As part of the city's underbelly, López dug through garbage for food and clothing like a scavenging mongrel. The gangs made strong bonds and protected each other; they had to learn to defend themselves and learn how to survive. According to Alexandra de la Torre Jaramillo, a criminal psychologist, these kids left their homes because they were abused, and they had no other option but to live on the streets. López said: 'I was a very alert child, very spirited with an innocent mind. My life has been dishonest because of being abandoned.' These gangs would also smoke bazuco, a drug derived from cocaine. López would hide out during the day, paranoid of strangers, and hunted for food when darkness fell. Within a year, the child of the night left his hometown and made his way to Bogotá, Colombia's sprawling, high-altitude capital.

It was a whole new world for López, home to popular museums including the Museo Botero, showcasing Fernando Botero's art, and the Museo del Oro, displaying pre-Columbian gold pieces. An American couple took pity on the desperately thin, starving wretch of a child and brought him to their home, enrolling him in a school for orphans. His good fortune did not last, however, because when he turned 12, López claimed he was molested by a male teacher. A short time later he stole money from the school office and ran away from the couple who'd taken him in, fleeing to the city's streets. With little education and no skills to speak of, López survived by doing what he did best—begging for food and money and committing petty crimes. His thieving led him to stealing vehicles, and it proved a lucrative move for he soon found himself being well paid for selling on the stolen vehicles to chop shops. But when he was 18, he was arrested for car theft and sentenced to seven years' imprisonment. He had only been incarcerated a few days when he was gang-raped by two other inmates. For López it could be termed as the straw that broke the camel's back, for he vowed never to be violated again in his life. Revenge came swift and fast; he made a shiv and hunted down his rapists, killing them both. Deeming his actions as self-defence, the local Colombian justice department merely added a further two years to his sentence. The killings, however, gained López the grudging respect of fellow inmates, who never dared disturb him. López said: 'When I was locked up in Colombia, I was taught how to defend myself. I don't deny that I killed two others, but the warden said don't worry.'

Following his release, López became a drifter and began abducting, raping, and murdering an average of three young girls every week. Posing as a salesman, he picked on poor, indigenous children, relying on his charm to lure them away. In fact, he never actually kidnapped any of his victims; instead he would appear as if he was helpless so the innocent youngsters would trust him. He would then take them somewhere quiet, so they could not be heard if they screamed. López said he strangled them so they would go to heaven and not suffer in this world. Set on his murderous ways, he would satisfy his urges and his fantasies by killing over and over again. He later claimed that, by 1978, he had killed more than 100 children. On one occasion, López attempted to abduct a nine-year-old from the Ayachucos community, an Indian tribe, but was caught in the act. As a result, he was beaten, tortured and buried up to his neck by the natives, who planned to pour syrup on his head and let him be eaten alive by ants. An American Christian missionary who was living and ministering to the tribe pleaded with the leaders to spare López's life. The missionary stressed that the natives should turn over López to the Peruvian police authorities and follow the country's law, rather than take a vigilante justice approach. They relented. López left the tribe with the missionary, who handed him to the state police. The Peruvian authorities, however, deported him to his native Colombia without prosecuting him for any crimes.

Once back in the country, López strayed back and forth to Ecuador, abducting and murdering more girls. Police initially believed that slavery and prostitution rings were responsible for the abductions and did little in the way of investigating. Instead they sent out a release stating that the disappearances of the girls were because they had failed their school year. The families did what they could to find their daughters, placing advertisements in newspapers and posting on streetlamps, offering rewards for information—but no information was forthcoming. Then the bodies of some of the missing girls began to show up. They had been raped and strangled. When more young girls disappeared, families demanded answers. But the police had no leads and no suspects, nor was there any evidence to even begin to identify a suspect. The citizens of Ecuador grew wary because the killer could be anyone and could be anywhere.

The city of Ambato is located in the central Andean valley of Ecuador. Lying on the banks of the Ambato River, the capital of the province of Tungurahua nestles beneath several tall mountains and sits at 2,577 metres above sea level. Ambato is known for its Fiesta de Frutas y Flores (Festival of Fruits and Flowers), celebrating the resilience of the land and its people. Sunday, March 9, 1980, was just like any other day in Ambato. Fruit and vegetable vendors were busy setting out their stalls and people were busy preparing food. No one paid any attention to the stranger busy peddling chains, padlocks and other trinkets. The man strolled along the plaza for most of the day before approaching the stall run by Carlina Ramone at about 4pm. Inquiring about her food, his eye was actually on her 11-year-old daughter and he tried to grab her attention. Carlina was aware that young children had vanished in the area and, having become suspicious of the man, she and other vendors chased after him as he exited the plaza. They grabbed him and Carlina accused him of kidnapping and killing the little girls. López said he was merely a poor, humble man. 'I am not anything, I have a clean heart,' he insisted. The group was not convinced and held him until the police arrived. Subjected to a stand-ard interrogation, he told the authorities that he was not Ecuadorian but a Colombian drifter and a 'good person.' Captain Pastor Córdova took over the questioning, adopting a friendly approach and offering López food and cigarettes. He inquired as to his general health and wellbeing, before the questions moved on to more serious matters—was he able to offer any information about the gang of abductors believed to be responsible for the missing children? López merely shrugged and said he knew nothing about it. Captain Córdova explained that the authorities were under consid-erable pressure from the families of the missing girls. López opened up and said one victim could be found by a cabin on the outskirts of the town. The police duly attended and found the body of a child.

On May 5, 1980, the 12-year-old girl had been selling newspapers on the street. Her mother was pregnant, and the youngster was trying to save money to provide for her brother. López approached her and asked if she would be his guide in the city, giving her 10 sucre. He then led her to the outskirts of town where he raped, beat and strangled her, throwing her body into a ditch by a bridge. He covered her with the same newspapers that she had been selling. When the child failed to arrive home, her father, Leonidas Garces, went to look for her but to no avail. He later told a documentary: 'Oh how I was suffering for my daughter. The tortures he did. What he did. His terror. It was terrible for a father to see the horrors that he committed when you saw her. If I had a gun, I would have killed him, but there was a policeman on one side and a policeman on another side.' What the authorities had discovered was merely the beginning of the true horror that was about to unfold.

At first the public was unaware it was López who was leading police to the graves. The authorities escorted him in disguise because the public was intent on lynching the culprit; some even threw rocks at him before the police intervened. During further police questioning, López said he'd spent the previous seven years travelling through Colombia, Ecuador and Peru, during which time he had raped and murdered hundreds of young girls. The officers were stunned. Could it be possible that one man could have carried out so much violence? Having already admitted to 110 murders, the high number of victims made police sceptical. That was until a flash flood near Ambato uncovered a mass grave and the bodies of four missing children were uncovered. López's confessions set off a heartbreaking six weeks of searching for the bodies of his victims, as he led police across 11 Ecuadorian provinces.

Captain Córdova inquired as to exactly how many girls López had killed. 'Over 200 in Ecuador, some tens in Peru, and many more in Colombia,' came the reply. Having been informed of López's confession, the President of Ecuador, Jaime Roldós Aguilera, ordered that López be taken to the places where he had left the bodies until all of the victims in Ecuador were recovered. To keep him talking, López was given tobacco and coffee, and invited to eat chicken and drink beer. It did the trick: he did indeed continue to talk, remembering everything—the dates, the times and the descriptions of the girls. Throughout this time, he felt nothing. No remorse, no guilt, nothing, leading the police to more than 30 shallow graves, all containing girls aged nine to 12. At a grave in Salcedo, he grabbed a victim's skull and placed it under his arm so a picture could be taken of him proudly showing off his trophy. However, after hearing that he was going to be charged for murder, he stopped cooperating and instead declared himself innocent. 'Being a child, I lost my innocence, they dishonoured me,' he said, 'it was something I wanted to forget, but I don't deny it affected me. I have always wanted to punish those responsible.'

By this time the media had given López the nickname The Monster of the Andes. A total of 53 bodies were recovered in Ambato alone, even though many graves had been emptied by flash floods or scavenging animals before the investigators could find them. When López went to trial, victims' families thought justice would not be served; the authorities hardly ever considered the welfare of the poor. As for 33-year-old López, he knew that the laws of Ecuador would protect him. Whether he had killed one person or a thousand, he would receive the same sentence—16 years. The law did not allow for consecutive sentences. His would amount to four months for every girl he killed. On July 31, 1981, López pleaded guilty in an Ecuadorian court to the murders of 57 girls. He was imprisoned in Ambato and agreed to be interviewed by a local reporter. 'I can declare I,

Pedro Alonso López, out of these acts declare myself guilty,'
he said. Throughout the interview he tried to explain his
crimes. He claimed he was a killer because of the sexual
and physical abuse he'd suffered as a child. 'I allegedly took
away their innocence, but my innocence has been taken
away from me.' Psychologists believed his brutal crimes also
satisfied another twisted desire. One of the reasons he said
he killed the children was because his victims were poor,
and perhaps he felt them ugly or useless, and was therefore
was attempting to stamp out their weakness. This, in turn,
allowed him to feel stronger somehow. He had no social
recognition, so it was an opportunity for him to feel big, to
show the world what he was doing.

Curiously, López spoke of his victims as if he cared about
them, believing he had saved them from a life of misery. He
called them his dolls, as if he was on a kind of mission. On
other occasions he blamed an alternate personality, Jorge
Patino, for the murders. When asked how many crimes he
had committed, he responded: 'I did not commit, I partic-
ipated in the acts and was involved in them. He (Patino)
was threatening to kill me and if I left him, he would kill
me.' López underwent psychological evaluation in prison,
which determined that he was a sociopath and suffered from
an antisocial personality disorder. According to criminal
psychologist Alexandra de la Torre Jaramillo, he did not
consciously know right from wrong, which is why he never
felt guilt or remorse for what he had done: 'He was unable
to feel other people's pain or feelings. What he did, he did

for his own pleasure.' After having served only two years in prison in Ambato, López was transferred to Garcia Moreno prison in Quito and kept in Pabellon D, which is reserved for murderers and rapists. He passed his days alone, smoking basuko, scribbling in a diary and carving coins with Jesus on one side and the Devil on other. 'I have always lived in poverty and had ambition to be powerful one day or of great importance. I understand what I have done. There is no going back,' he said.

On August 31, 1994, he was released on good behaviour, having served 14 years of his 16-year stretch. But his stay in Ecuador was short-lived—he was detained after just one hour of freedom, having been ordered back into custody by the superintendent of the province for López to be deported to Colombia. According to the superintendent, López was an illegal and not in possession of proper documentation, and therefore he could not be set free. López attempted to stop his deportation, claiming that he'd gained Ecuadorian citizenship in 1974, but he could not produce any evidence of this. The following day, Ecuadorian immigration officials handed López over to Colombian authorities. Led out to the van, a waiting crowd chanted 'Die, die, die!' as he was driven to the border. Fearful that López would continue to murder the innocent, the country's national security department was not prepared to allow him to roam at will. Shortly after his arrival in Colombia he was handed over to prosecutors in the Colombian state of Golema, where it was hoped to take advantage of the country's harsher laws and put him away for good. In Bogota, López protested as he was subjected to a medical evaluation, demanding to be set free, even as an angry mob had gathered outside with the intention of lynching him. However, nobody had ever charged López for murder in Colombia. Still reluctant to set him free, the authorities moved him to El Espinal, where he had resided decades earlier with his mother, in the hope that one of his older victims would come forward.

A local woman named Alba Sánchez claimed that in 1979, she had seen López walk away with her daughter Floralba from her home, before her body was found raped and strangled in a rural area outside town. The modus operandi was identical to López's documented murders in Ecuador. He was duly charged but again managed to dodge a bullet. In late 1995 he was declared insane and sent to the psychiatric wing of Quito's García Moreno prison in Bogotá, where he became a model prisoner and met Colombian paedophile serial killer Daniel Camargo. In February 1998 a prison psychiatrist declared him sane. A mere $50 bail saw him freed with two conditions: he had to continue receiving psychiatric treatment, and he had to report once a month to a judge. He did neither. Instead he absconded.

The news of López's release caused hysteria in Ecuador. It was rumoured that he had been seen in the northern part of the country around this time, but this was never confirmed. López was next seen again in El Espinal, when he knocked on the door of his mother, Benilda. 'The day he came to me he said, Mother, kneel down in front of me so I can bless you, and I said the one who should kneel down is you. The son is the one who kneels before his mother. He got down on only one knee,' she told a documentary. López told Benilda that he had come to see her about inheritance. She replied that she was poor and how could she give him anything when all she had was a chair and a bed? López took the items and placed them on the porch and as his mother began to cry, López said: 'Who will buy this? If not, I will light them on fire.' A woman bought the chair and the small bed, and with that López left, having pocketed the money. He returned to the countryside he knew so well—back to the killing fields, never to be seen again. In a televised interview, his mother later admitted that she thought her son was going to kill her because he had blamed her 'for every pain in [his] heart', and she had pleaded for López to never be released. In 2002, the Colombian police launched an Interpol order of arrest against López for a new murder in El Espinal that fitted the modus operandi of his early crimes. Rumours claimed he was living in Tolima Department, Colombia, as a homeless man in Bogota and even that he was murdered after some relatives of his victims had placed a bounty on his head.

López had deliberately targeted young girls aged between eight and 12, mostly from poor, rural Amerindian communities. He had no racial preference and admitted to having been tempted at times to abduct Caucasian girls, including foreign tourists, but refrained from doing so because usually they were more closely watched by their parents. He would stalk the girls, abduct them and take them to a secluded place, where he would rape and then strangle them to death. Afterwards, he would bury their bodies in shallow graves, in groups of three or four. Before the bodies decomposed too much, he would return and play 'tea parties' with groups of corpses. He would bring new victims to graves he'd already prepared while they were still alive, and those graves were sometimes filled with the dead bodies of other girls. Adopting his usual approach of soft, reassuring, comforting words, he would keep the child calm throughout the night. As the sun rose over the horizon, he would rape and strangle them. He never killed his victims at night. To López, that would have been a waste because he would not have been able to see his victim's eyes as their life ebbed away.

According to Dr. Dirk Gibson, of the University of New Mexico, who wrote about López in his book Serial Killers Around the World: The Global Dimensions of Serial Murder, López shared a common trait with many serial killers: a horrific childhood. 'Lopez claimed his murders were revenge for the gang rape he suffered in prison, and because of the mistreatment from his mother,' he wrote. 'It was believed those children were human trafficked, stolen or sold on the market or that they ran away. Often local law enforcement suspected serial killers last. In general, a serial killer will continue to kill until he's stopped.' It had taken a natural disaster to literally uncover López's crimes. But save for the bodies found, his claimed death toll should be taken with a grain of salt, Dr. Gibson said. 'Many, if not most exaggerate their victim count. These aren't exactly honest people, and they are interested in glory, so they inflate their crimes. But at the very least, he killed up to 70 people.' López never showed remorse for his crimes. In a prison interview with journalist Ron Laytner in 1994, he said if he ever got out of jail, he would happily return to killing. The pleasure he received from his demented acts overpowered any sense of right from wrong, and he looked forward to the opportunity to wrap his hands around the throat of his next child. In one three-year period, he was averaging three victims a week, luring them away from markets with trinkets. 'I walked among the markets searching for a girl with a certain look on her face. A look of innocence and beauty,' he told Laytner. 'She would be a good girl, always working with her mother. I followed them, sometimes for two or three days, waiting for the moment when she was left alone.'

The FBI defines a serial killer as one who murders three or more victims, with cooling-off periods in between. This sets them apart from mass murderers, who kill four or more people at the same time or in a short period of time, in the same place, and spree killers, who murder in multiple locations and within a short period of time. Serial killers usually work alone, kill strangers and kill for the sake of killing, as opposed to crimes of passion. According to an FBI study, there have been about 400 serial killers in the U.S. in the past century, with anywhere from 2,526 to 3,860 victims. Other studies have examined why someone becomes a serial killer. There are three possible theories: childhood neglect and abuse, mental illness and brain injury. Pedro López would fit into the second scenario, having been subjected to neglect and abuse as a child. An FBI study which involved interviewing dozens of serial killers identified 'similar patterns of severe childhood neglect'. During a child's development, there are important periods in which they learn about love, trust, empathy and basic rules about how to interact with other human beings. If these traits aren't imprinted upon the child during that period, it may not be possible for them to learn them later in life.

A serial killer keeps killing until one of four things happens: they are caught, they die, they kill themselves or they burn out. It is frightening and disturbing that whatever happened to the Monster of the Andes is unknown. Many hope that one of the many bounties offered for his death eventually paid off. However, if López is still alive, there is the lingering realisation that he may well still be killing. When news of his capture first hit the airwaves, López relished the attention and was not shy about discussing his crimes or philosophising about life and death on camera. 'When one dies one totally loses his emotions, his vision, his ability to see, a death that you can forget who you are, everything you did is now darkness,' he said. López hoped to gain a twisted kind of immortality. 'This will be history, right?' he asked a reporter, 'Will it be important? I'm too young to die, man. I am a god, I give life, and I can take it away. I am the worst of the worst. Perhaps I took it too far because of my ignorance. The lowest of the low. Perhaps even a complete animal.'

CHAPTER 11

HARVEY AND JEANNETTE CREWE

'There is blood all over the place and I cannot find them anywhere.'—Lenard Demler.

N EW ZEALAND'S longest river, the Waikato, winds a leisurely 260 miles from Lake Taupo on the Central Plateau to the Tasman Sea. Extending across the upper part of the North Island, Waikato is a region rich in diversity. In the early part of the 20th century most of the hill country was developed for farming, and today it is one of the richest agricultural and pastoral areas of the world, home to New Zealand's famous dairy and thoroughbred horse racing industries. The rural tranquility and views of farmland and bush have made it increasingly popular for lifestyle living, with many migrants making Waikato their home. The region's largest city is Hamilton, where residents and visitors enjoy some of the most spectacular gardens in the country, including the international award-winning Hamilton Gardens, an internationally-recognised zoo, one of New Zealand's largest aquatic centres and world-class international sports stadiums. Extensive walkways and cycleways link the city's residential areas to the beautiful Waikato River, which flows right through the city.

Located in the Lower Waikato River area of the Waikato District, Pukekawa is one of the oldest volcanic cones in the Auckland region. The area's fertile soil is perfect for growing vegetables, including onions, potatoes and carrots. The area also spawned a reputation for violence. On the night of August 24, 1920, farmer Sydney Seymour Eyre was shot dead in his home in the north Waikato farming hamlet. He had been in the bedroom with his wife when an unknown assailant fired a shotgun through an open window. Eyre was running a flourishing sheep farm, and with a wife and five children, he had no enemies to speak of. Police were quickly on the case, discovering cartridges and hoof marks, suggesting the murderer had fled on horseback. That led them to a former employee on the Eyre farm, Samuel Thorn. Detectives checked the shoes of more than 1,300 horses before they found Mickey, a draught horse on the farm of James Grenville. Grenville had recently taken on a new farm hand, Samuel Thorn, who had the horse in his possession. He also had a recently fired shotgun and several boxes of an uncommon brand of shotgun cartridges—the same brand as a wrapper found outside Eyre's bedroom window. Thorn was convicted of murder by the Auckland Supreme Court and hanged, despite protesting his innocence until he drew his final breath. The trial was a national sensation. Fifty years later, the facts of the case would prove eerily similar to the murder of couple Harvey and Jeannette Crewe.

According to the Global Peace Index, a report published annually by the Institute for Economics and Peace, New Zealand is the second safest country in the world after Iceland. Pukekawa is probably no different to anywhere else in the country. By 1970, it was an affluent rural community and service centre of several hundred people. Farming, the mainstay of the region, was in a state of constant flux, shifting through the decades from Maori horticulture to dairying and back to horticulture and market gardening. In the summer of 1970, Pukekawa was thrust into the limelight—sheep farmers David Harvey and Jeannette Lenore Crewe, had been shot to death in the living room of their home, and their bodies unceremoniously dumped in the Waikato River. It took five days before anyone realised what had happened; their 18-month-old daughter Rochelle was found home alone, sitting in her crib. Bread, milk and newspaper deliveries had piled up. Multiple bloodstains were discovered in the property, and brain matter too.

Jeannette Lenore Crewe was born into a farming family. Her parents Lenard and May Demler married in 1936. The following year Lenard purchased a 465-acre farm in Sharpe Road, Pukekawa, which the couple farmed together. Their land was situated adjacent to his brother-in-law, Howard Chennell's 340-acre farm. Some years later, Lenard experienced problems involving unpaid taxes to the Inland Revenue Department and acting on advice from his accountant, he sold half of the farm to his wife to minimise their future tax obligations. Jeannette was born on February 6, 1940, and two years later May gave birth to their second daughter, Dianne Heather. The girls grew up on the farm and attended the local Pukekawa Primary School, prior to receiving a private school education at St Cuthbert's College in Epsom, Auckland. In 1950, their Uncle Howard was killed in a tractor accident on his farm, and the girls were bequeathed his farm in equal shares. The farm became known as the Chennell Estate and was run by a series of resident farm managers until the sisters reached the age of 25. Meanwhile, Jeannette trained as a teacher at Ardmore Teachers' Training College in 1957 and qualified the following year. She then worked at a number of places in the North Island. In 1961 and 1962 she travelled overseas, returning to New Zealand in 1963 to hold a brief relief teaching position at Maramarua District High School and Pakakura Intermediate. This was followed by a position at Wanganui. During this time, she formed a relationship with Harvey Crewe, at that time a 22-year-old stock agent.

David Harvey Crewe, known by his middle name, had a similar background to Jeannette. He was born on October 20, 1941 and raised in a farming district in the lower North Island, attending school in Wellington. After leaving

education, he was employed on various farms in the Wood-
ville and Wanganui districts and spent two years as a shepherd in the Kumeroa area, employed by his friend from his
teenage years, Graham Hewson. Jeannette was living and
teaching in Wanganui when she met him. The couple wed
on June 18, 1966, at St George Church, in Ranfurly Road,
Epsom, Auckland. Prior to the marriage, Harvey arranged to
purchase a half share in the Chennell property from Heather,
who was by then resident in the U.S. The sale completed on
August 1966, with an agreed sum of NZ$40,000. Harvey
paid $9,000 from savings and obtained a State Advances
mortgage for the remaining balance. Jeannette's parents still
owned and occupied the adjoining 465-acre farm. Determined to increase the efficiency and profitability of their
farm, located some 60 yards off Highway 22, the newlyweds
set to the 340-acre plot with vigour. The hardworking couple
appeared content and happy, and were successful farmers,
running both sheep and beef stock.

Life was not all sunshine and roses: in 1967 their home was
burgled, during which jewellery and other personal property
belonging to Jeannette was stolen. On December 1, 1968,
Rochelle was born. Six days after the birth, the family was
absent from the property when a fire occurred in a spare
bedroom. It was supposed that the blaze was caused by a
cigarette or an electrical fault, but Harvey and Jeannette
believed it was arson. Six months later, on May 28, 1969, a
hay barn on the property near the farmhouse was destroyed
by fire. A passing motorist, David Fleming, informed Harvey

but by the time he got there, the structure was beyond salvage, as were the 800 bales of hay stored inside. Again, the cause was not definitively established, but it was ruled as spontaneous combustion. In February 1970 Jeannette's mother died of a brain tumour and her father continued to live by himself at his farm on Highway 22, becoming a regular visitor to the Crewe household for meals. Probate in relation to his wife's estate bequeathed her share of the Demler farm to Jeannette, together with money, shareholdings and personal belongings including a motor vehicle. Amended terms of her will specified that her husband had the right to occupy the whole farm and derive full income from it during his lifetime. Under the terms of the will, almost $23,000 was to be paid to Lenard to satisfy the mortgage debt, with the balance of May's estate bequested to Jeannette. Younger daughter Heather had been cut out of her mother's will because she married a divorced father of three. A strict Presbyterian, May Demler had not approved of the union.

On June 17, 1970, Harvey and Jeannette were murdered. The killing took place in the evening, said the police, because the couple had been seen during the day running errands. The investigation also documented reports of a woman, who was never officially identified, in the Crewe household before they were reported as missing, apparently having fed Rochelle and the farm's animals. On June 22, at 2.20pm, Constable Wyllie, of the Tuakau Police, answered a call from Lenard Demler's alarmed neighbour, Owen Priest. He had been to Harvey and Jeannette's home. There were bloodstains in the house and their infant daughter was all alone—the couple were missing. The events actually unfolded like this: a transport company agent had been telephoning the couple but got no answer. He alerted Lenard Demler, who visited his daughter and son-in-law's house. He noticed bloodstains in the lounge and his granddaughter, alone, in her cot. He left the child behind and drove back to his home, where he telephoned the agent, telling them not to bother sending a truck to collect livestock because Harvey was not at home. He then drove to Owen Priest's house, telling him: 'There is blood all over the place and I cannot find them anywhere.' Priest accompanied Lenard to the farmhouse. There, Lenard collected Rochelle from her cot and Priest drove them home, before he himself drove 7km to the home of district nurse Barbara Willis, asking for her help with looking after the child. He also called the police.

Meanwhile, three other significant inquiries were taking place: the murders of Jennifer Beard, in Southland, and Oliver Walker and Betty McKay in the Bay of Plenty. The investigators involved were under considerable pressure to wrap them up. With a fourth investigation to contend with—and with no immediate indication as to where Harvey and Jeannette were, or who was responsible for their absence—there was yet more pressure on the force. Detective Inspector Bruce Hutton was put in charge of this particular investigation. He arrived at the scene at 5.10pm, shortly after Priest's call, with Detective Senior Sergeant Schultz and a police photographer. A thorough investigation was conducted over the following weeks but offered no results. Though it seemed likely that Harvey and Jeannette were dead, no bodies were found, nor was there any immediate indications as to who the culprit was: Jeannette's father, Lenard Demler, was Hutton's initial suspect, but there was no sufficient evidence either way.

A development occurred two months later, on August 16, when Jeannette Crewe's body was found in the Waikato River at a place called Devil's Elbow. She had been wrapped in a blanket and bound with copper wire. Fifteen fragments from a .22 bullet wound to her head were recovered, and one large fragment had the number 8 embossed on the base. The samples were immediately sent to the Department of Scientific and Industrial Research for comparison with bullets test-fired from 64 registered .22 firearms—barely three per cent of the total recorded as held in the Pukekawa area. The registered rifles were collected from relatives and associates of the Crewes, and from residents within five miles of their farm. An intense search for a .22 cartridge case was conducted in the house and enclosure, both of which had already been carefully searched on June 22. A forensic report released to Hutton on August 19 stated that of the 64 firearms examined, all but two were eliminated as the possible murder weapon. One of the remaining two belonged to Pukekawa farmer John Eyre, and was not eliminated until 1980, when further tests were carried out as part of a Royal Commission of Inquiry review: the Eyre rifle bullets were shown to have five lands and grooves, not six. Research shows nothing to suggest any member of the Eyre family was ever interviewed by the police. Mickey Eyre had worked for Harvey Crewe but was apparently twice thrown off the property by Harvey in a violent rage. Mickey had a disability which prevented him from speaking, and his mother claimed he never went out unaccompanied at night because of it. This turned out to be untrue: local people reported seeing Mickey out and about in the area at night, with a gun. Once he was discovered on someone's porch late at night, carrying a .22 rifle. The other firearm belonged to Arthur Thomas.

Arthur Allan Thomas was born in 1938 and had four brothers and four sisters. He was raised on his parents' 272-acre dairy farm at Mercer Ferry Road, eight miles away from the Crewes. He left school aged 14 to work with his father on the farm, followed by a job at an uncle's farm. He then began labouring at Roose Shipping Company, and also spent some time in Maramarua as a forestry worker, later as an employee of Barr Brothers, an aerial top-dressing firm. In November 1964 he wed Vivien Carter, who'd recently arrived from England and was staying with her uncle in Wellsford. After the marriage he worked on a number of farms until June 1966, when he entered into a five-year lease with his father to take over the family farm at Pukekawa. Thomas was initially questioned on July 2, 1970, at his home in Mercer Ferry Valley by Detective Sergeant Hughes. Beverley Willis had told them how her friend Jeannette had, prior to 1961, been pestered by a local boy—and Thomas was fingerprinted at the time. He was then visited by Detective Parkes on August 12 and shown a card attached to a brush, comb and mirror set found in the Crewe's house. Thomas stated that he had given it to Jeanette as a gift years before, in 1962.

A month after Jeannette's body was recovered, Harvey Crewe was found upriver, shot in the head with a .22 bullet and, exactly like his wife, wrapped in a blanket and bound with copper wire. A car axle was in the water near the body, and officers believed it had been used to weigh Harvey's body down. The axle was later identified as coming from a 1928/9 model Nash motorcar series 420. Post-mortem examinations on both bodies confirmed they had been murdered on June 17. On September 7, Thomas was interviewed at Tuakau Police Station and told his rifle had discharged the lethal bullets. Thomas denied any involvement. After the interview, Detective Parkes stated: '… both Detective Sergeant Seaman and myself are convinced that he is not involved in this inquiry.' The following day, his rifle was returned to the custody of his wife, Vivien, and the Eyre family rifle was also returned to them. Skip to October 13, and Detective Johnson visited Thomas and showed him a car axle. When asked about its origin, Thomas said he'd never seen it before. On October 20, police attended his home and took possession of the rifle they'd returned. The following day, police searched the Crewe farm again and discovered a .22 cartridge in a garage on the property. This was later found to contain a bullet with the number eight embossed on the base. There was more: the car axle found

in the river near Harvey's body had apparently been identified as having been in use on a trailer owned by Thomas's
father, and tests carried out on copper wire at his farm was
deemed as a good to excellent match for the wire used to
wrap the bodies. On October 22, Thomas made a statement about his associations with Jeannette years before, his
movements on the evening of June 17, the axle found with
Harvey's body, his .22 Browning rifle, wire samples taken
from his farm, blood found on overalls in the boot of his
vehicle, and why he did not help the police in searching for
the Crewes. On October 27, Detective Sergeant Charles and
Detective Sergeant Parkes searched the flower bed opposite
the kitchen window at the crime scene—despite the area
already having been meticulously gridsearched. DS Charles
located a .22 cartridge; markings on the shell casing were
consistent with it having been fired by Thomas's rifle. He
was interviewed at his home on the same day.

Thomas was arrested and charged with murdering the
Crewes on November 11. He was remanded in custody until
another appearance on November 25, and then again to
December 14 at the Otahuhu Magistrates' Court for the
taking of depositions. The Lower Court hearing lasted until
December 22, when evidence was heard from 84 witnesses.
With a prima facie case established, Thomas was committed
to the Supreme Court for trial on both charges, presided
over by Justice Trevor Henry. The eleven-day hearing began
on February 15, 1971, during which evidence was heard
from 101 witnesses. Thomas's defence counsel, Paul Temm,

assisted by Brian Webb, told the court Thomas was at home with Vivien and his cousin Peter Thomas at the time of the murders; an alibi corroborated by both Vivien and Peter, and which was never contradicted by other evidence. Prosecuting, Auckland Crown Solicitor David Morris, assisted by David Baragwanath, suggested the mysterious woman seen at the Crewe's house around the time of the crime was Vivien, though no charge was forthcoming. To this day, who cared for Rochelle in the farmhouse remains a mystery. When the child was put into the care of neighbour Mrs Willis, she was hungry but not starving. Mrs Willis, a district nurse, looked her over and, apart from nappy rash, Rochelle was in good health. Later, two paediatricians examined her and found she had lost a little weight during those five days but had certainly been fed. Evidence at the house also proved that someone had changed her nappy, probably a number of times. The jury found Thomas guilty on both counts and he was sentenced to life imprisonment. On May 4 he lodged an appeal against conviction, which was dismissed by the Court of Appeal on June 18.

Meanwhile, a campaign had been set up by a group of Thomas's supporters, determined to bring to public attention anomalies in the original investigation. They claimed the cartridge found in the garden of Harvey and Jeannette's home had been planted by two of the investigating officers in the case. In late 1971, a petition was submitted by Allan Thomas and Patrick Vesey, of the Arthur Thomas Retrial Committee Inc., to the Governor-General, seeking a new trial. The material was considered by Sir George McGregor, a retired judge of the Supreme Court. His report, dated February 2, 1972, stated that, in his opinion, there had been no miscarriage of justice. However, after a further petition on June 2, the matter was put before the Court of Appeal. Evidence and submissions were heard over four days and on February 26, 1973, the Court of Appeal ordered a second trial. It began on March 27 and lasted until April 13, when Thomas was again convicted of both murders and sentenced to life imprisonment. The prosecution said the motive was Thomas's obsession with Jeannette, but little evidence was offered to back that up—apart from Lenard Demler testifying that Thomas had pestered his daughter. Nor was there any real investigation into who else might have had access to the car axle found in the water near Harvey's body. Police had identified the axle as being on a trailer owned by Thomas's father, but only up until August 1965—five years before the murders. Another appeal was lodged against his second conviction but was dismissed on July 11. Less than two weeks later, on July 27, a total of 125 exhibits in the case were disposed of—an action which resulted in significant criticism of the police and a stinging rebuke from the Minister of Justice, Dr. Martin Finlay, who was 'deeply troubled.' At the insistence of Assistant Commissioner Walton, police tried to recover the exhibits from where they had been dumped at Whitford Tip, but the task proved impossible.

In 1978, the late British author David Yallop—who had written two books on miscarriages of justice—took an interest in Thomas. He spent more than a year in New Zealand investigating the case and became convinced Thomas was innocent. In an open letter to New Zealand's Prime Minister, he demanded Thomas's release on the grounds that he 'has not been found guilty beyond reasonable doubt. He has in fact been found innocent beyond reasonable doubt.' The nature and seriousness of the allegations were such that Prime Minister Robert Muldoon appointed Mr. Adams-Smith QC to report to him. While the courts had been satisfied of Thomas's guilt, sections of the public remained unconvinced. For the first time, the integrity of the police became widely questioned and a campaign challenging the safety of the conviction was launched, driven in large part by the Auckland Star newspaper. Campaigners believed that the police had planted the shell casing. Cue industrial chemist Jim Sprott, who forensically analysed the casing. His examinations showed that the casing's condition was too good to have been in the garden for as long as the police claimed it had been, and the bullets found in Harvey and Jeannette's bodies had been manufactured at a different time to the casings. Thus, it was impossible that they had come from the same shell casing at all. And what of the car axle reputedly found near Harvey Crewe's body? It had indeed been on the Thomas farm, but had been taken away by vintage car enthusiasts and later dumped on the roadside close the Eyre family farm, some years before the murders.

Arthur Thomas, who had lost his freedom, his farm, his reputation and his marriage, was granted a free pardon by Governor-General Sir Keith Hoylake, on December 17, 1979, on the recommendation of the Prime Minister, and was immediately released from prison. He received NZ$1,087,450.35 compensation for the time he served in jail and for the loss of the use of the farm. Yallop wrote a book about his investigation, called Beyond Reasonable Doubt. In 1980 a Royal Commission of Inquiry (RCOI) reviewed the circumstances of Thomas's convictions, including questioning if the investigation by the police was carried out properly and if there was any impropriety during the inquiry. They also reviewed if there were any matters that should have investigated and were not, whether proper steps were taken after Thomas's arrest to investigate any information which suggested that he was not responsible for the murders, whether the arrest and prosecution was justified, and whether the prosecution failed at any stage to perform any duty it owed to the defence in respect of the disclosure of evidentiary material which might have assisted the defence.

The commission found that the cartridge case discovered in the garden—and relied on to convict Thomas—was created by a bullet fired from Thomas's gun after it was seized by the police. Detective Inspector Bruce Hutton, the Officer-In-Charge of the investigation, and one of his team, Detective Lenrick Johnston, were guilty of corruption. During the second trial, they had fabricated evidence by planting a cartridge case in the garden, and Hutton exchanged a case found on Thomas's farm with another matching the one in the garden. Thomas's wrongful nine-year imprisonment, the commission said, was a wrong that could never be put right and 'the high-handed and oppressive actions of those responsible for his convictions cannot be obliterated.' The arrest and prosecution of Thomas was wholly unjustified, they said, and the officers' conduct—faking evidence and lying on oath to incriminate Thomas—was an 'unspeakable outrage': 'The fact that he was imprisoned on the basis of evidence which was false to the knowledge of police officers, whose duty it is to uphold the law, is an unspeakable outrage. Such action is no more and no less than a shameful and cynical attack on the trust that all New Zealanders have and are entitled to have in their police force and system of administration of justice. Mr. Thomas suffered that outrage; he was the victim of that attack. His courage and that of a few very dedicated men and women who believed in the cause of justice has exposed the wrongs, which were done. They can never be put right.' Despite this, New Zealand Police never laid charges against any officer involved in the investigation and prosecution, and neither did the commission ever find out why Thomas was framed. Lenrick Johnston had died in 1978, and Bruce Hutton died in 2013.

Fast forward to the afternoon of November 19, 2010. An explosion ripped through the remote Pike River mine on the west coast of New Zealand's South Island, killing 29 men. It was during this most tragic of weeks, with the public's mind focused on the unfolding events, that the Government chose to release a press release turning down a request by Rochelle Crewe and Arthur Thomas for an

independent inquiry into the murders of Harvey and Jeannette. A month previously, author and investigative journalist Ian Wishart published a comprehensive analysis of the
murders in his book, Arthur Allan Thomas: The Inside Story.
Its publication prompted Rochelle—who was brought up
by Jeannette's sister, Heather, who returned home from the
U.S. after the murders—to ask for the case to be reopened
but the Government claimed it had no powers to direct the
police to reinvestigate. Having said that, it did have powers
to order a Commission of Inquiry, as it had done in the
past. No inquiry was forthcoming. But because Rochelle
demanded to know what further investigative action had
been taken after Thomas's pardon, and why Hutton and
Johnston had not been prosecuted, the then Police Commissioner, Howard Broad, appointed a small team of senior
investigators and analysts to undertake a review. There
followed four years of work: reviewing existing evidence
and other material from court and police files, archives and
publications; approaching and interviewing witnesses who
had already made statements and/or given evidence, as well
as additional potential witnesses; identifying and pursuing,
where possible, any further lines of inquiry; and obtaining
further expert opinion and analysis in relation to forensic
and specialist topics.

One of the several key findings in the 2014 Crewe Homicide Investigation Review by New Zealand Police was that
insufficient priority was given by the 1970 investigative
team to examine the inquiries made when the couple were

burgled in 1967 or the farmhouse fire in 1968 and the barn fire in 1969. The murder scene was poorly managed from the outset, therefore compromising its overall integrity. Of particular note was that the Officer-In-Charge had not been appointed for 24 hours after the police had been alerted: an investigative shortfall. The level of forensic awareness on the part of the investigators was deficient, and as a result, scene contamination, scene photography, fingerprint examination, exhibit seizure, security and handling were all adversely affected. Also, initial scene reconstructions failed to fully explore all possible scenarios, which therefore resulted in an inadequate search of the Crewe farmhouse and surrounds being carried out.

Notwithstanding the RCOI findings regarding Hutton and Johnston's actions, it concluded there was insufficient evidence to support a prosecution against any individual for a crime associated with corruption. Further re-investigation was not warranted, it said, because a legal opinion given in 1981 by Solicitor-General Paul Neazor—that there was insufficient evidence to implicate any individual for fabricating the provenance of the cartridge case found in the garden—still stood, because the evidence had not changed. Also, neither the two Supreme Court trial judges in Thomas's prosecution nor on the RCOI review had deemed the testimonies presented in court by witnesses as acts of perjury.

Tragically, the real murderer of Harvey and Jeannette Crewe has never been caught—and there are many unanswered questions. Who was the mysterious woman seen at their home? Why did Lenard Demler leave it so long to rescue Rochelle from the scene? A number of theories have been put forward over the years. One was that Harvey assaulted his wife, who then shot him, dumped his body with help from her father and several days later shot herself, and her father disposed of her body. Thomas's brother, Des, believes a local man must have been the killer. Another—that Lenard Demler killed them—was covered extensively in Chris Birt's book, The Final Chapter, in 2001. Journalist Ian Wishart agrees with Birt in rejecting the murder-suicide theory but doesn't believe Lenard was involved. Instead, he proposes two new suspects: the son of a prominent New Zealand family who worked in the area (Wishart does not directly name him), or one of the policemen who planted evidence to convict Thomas.

In July 2014, another review into the murders, at a cost of $400,000, cleared the late Lenard and his second wife, Norma, of any wrongdoing. Interestingly, it suggested that Rochelle hadn't eaten in those five days she was alone, and that the witness who saw a strange woman at the farm during that period was mistaken. Thomas, it said, was the sole suspect. A spokesman said: 'On release of the review report, police said that we were open to any significant and credible new information and this position remains unchanged. To date no such information has been brought to the attention of police.'

According to Amy Mass, writing for the stuff.co.nz website on October 30, 2015, a star witness for the prosecution in this notorious cold case was questioned by police over the discovery of bloodstained guns on his Coromandel Bach (beach house to non-New Zealanders) at the time of the Crewe murders. By all accounts, Rod Rasmussen found three guns—a shotgun, a 303 and a .22 rifle—under a water tank on his Coromandel Bach before the murders and turned them over to the police two days later. He remembered that one of the guns was stained with what looked like blood. Rasmussen stated that the only time the police asked him about the guns was in the past year, after he was accused by a relative of murdering the Crewes. As the star witness in the case for the Crown that secured the conviction of Thomas, Rasmussen stated that in 1965 he'd repaired a trailer belonging to the Thomas family. He had removed and replaced a stub axle on the trailer, and said he'd given it back to the family—something the family denied. Nothing happened and no steps were taken following the publication of Mass's article.

At the local Tuakau cemetery are the graves of Arthur Thomas's parents. Twenty-seven metres away lay the neglected graves of the Crewes—Jeannette's name wrongly spelt, as Jeanette. Rochelle Crewe maintains that crucial mistakes made by police, and that missed opportunities in the original investigation mean her parents' murders may never be solved. In a media conference following the publication of the Crewe Homicide Investigation Review, Grant Nicholls, the Acting Deputy Commissioner, said: 'No new information has come to light that would prompt police to initiate further inquiries that could realistically identify the offender. I am very mindful that we have not been able to answer the one question that she (Rochelle) wanted. I have apologised to her for shortfalls in the original investigation. The review was thorough, it was meticulous, and it was painstaking. It took a long time and it was done under the guidance of an individual Queen's Counsel, so I think the media and public can have a high degree of confidence in this review. If someone was to come forward today with critical evidence and information that was reliable, we would certainly consider it. We owe it to New Zealand, we owe it to Rochelle and we owe it to Jeannette and Harvey. So, if someone has information they have been hanging on to for in excess of 44 years, we would certainly like to hear from them.' Rochelle was satisfied that the review had 'exhausted all avenues' of the available evidence.

CHAPTER 12

SUZANNE ARMSTRONG AND SUSAN BARTLETT

*'We'll never really get over this until this fellow is caught.
You walk around not knowing who did the murder. It
could be the bloke next door."—Gayle Armstrong.*

MARVELLOUS MELBOURNE was a popular way
to describe the city. Situated in Victoria, in the
south-eastern part of mainland Australia, today
it is recognised for its many laneways, cultural diversity,
excellent dining options for all budgets and amazing street
art. It is also known for being the coffee capital of the world
and is regularly voted as the world's most livable city.

The 1970s, which saw the construction of Melbourne's
City Loop, was a period of protest and unrest, when battles
were lost against large-scale development. The largest

demonstrations were the Vietnam Moratoriums of 1970 and 1971, and the Labour rallies after the Whitlam Dismissal in 1975. Environmental protests also attracted large-scale support, particularly the anti-uranium mining demonstrations. On the economic front, unemployment stood at 1.8 per cent. After a turbulent decade for the economy, including a mid-decade recession, this figure had pushed northwards to six per cent by 1980. But it was not all doom and gloom. Platform shoes and flared trousers were in fashion, Margaret Court and Ken Rosewall were gracing the world tennis circuit, cassette tapes were the latest tech device, rock bands such as Led Zeppelin played Kooyong Stadium and the city was entertained by legendary crooner Frank Sinatra. Later in the decade, Swedish pop sensation Abba took the city by storm, performing at the Sidney Myer Music Bowl in 1977—a year that was also memorable for another, darker, reason.

Suzanne Armstrong and Susan Bartlett were both born in 1949 in Benalla, a small, rural town on the Broken River up country from Melbourne. The girls would have been told about Benalla's history: the town was famous for the Battle of Broken River (also known as the Faithfull Massacre), which took place in 1838 when 20 aboriginal Australians attacked 18 European settlers, killing seven. The girls met as 14-year-old high school pupils in 1963. Both were the eldest children from single-parent households. Sue's mother, Elaine, raised her daughter and younger brother on her own. Suzanne's parents divorced and, as the oldest of four children, she became largely responsible for the care of her siblings. The teenagers shared a love of music, and particularly enjoyed listening to The Beatles. When the group announced concert dates at Melbourne's Festival Hall in June 1964, the girls were overjoyed. The only problem was that the city was more than 120 miles away, and neither parent was interested in taking them. So, the girls purchased bus tickets instead.

Later, Suzanne spent a period abroad. She returned home to Australia in late 1973 and hoped to reunite with her childhood friend, but Sue herself was out of the country. Sue had left her teaching job in Broadford to enjoy an extended holiday in Greece. The friends exchanged letters, and it was decided that Suzanne would fly out to Greece to join her friend. Low on funds, she secured a job as a taxi driver, saving madly to buy the plane ticket. The pair eventually met up in Athens and set off on a tour of the Greek islands. When they arrived in Naxos in late 1974, Suzanne caught the eye of a young fisherman and they became romantically involved. In January 1975, Sue gained employment as an arts and crafts teacher at Collingwood High School and returned to Australia for the new term, initially living in the neighbourhood of Richmond. She was happy in her new position and was enjoying life. While Sue taught class, Suzanne—now pregnant—stayed with her lover in Naxos. But things didn't work out as she had hoped. The couple discussed marriage, but Suzanne quickly become frustrated with the bureaucracy she faced as a foreigner. After the birth of their son, Gregory, she found that what had once been a paradise was turning into a prison. By 1976, she decided to return to Australia with Gregory for Christmas, with the intention of heading to Melbourne. She had also been in contact with Sue, and the two agreed that it would be perfect for them to move in together.

By this time, the effects of the 1973-1974 American stock market crash were being felt in Australia, resulting in a fall in employment and property prices. Sue, Suzanne and toddler Gregory settled in Collingwood, one of the oldest suburbs of Melbourne, notable for its historical buildings and converted warehouses, which today house offices, galleries, cafés and quirky shops. Once demonised as an area of poverty and disadvantage, the older workers' cottages, so much a part of the fabric of the place, had made way for high-rise public housing estates in the late 1960s. Collingwood continued to be characterised by population fluctuations and demographic change, which had witnessed a shift in the community from a largely British ancestry to a diversity of ethnicities, driven by waves of immigration. Greeks, Italians, Macedonians, Lebanese and Vietnamese settled here and began to raise families, seeing Australian-born residents falling to half the population.

The rents were still affordable, and it meant a shorter commute to school for Sue. Once they were settled, along came a new addition to the family in the shape of Mishka, a shepherd cross puppy. Late October 1976 was particularly warm, and the new roommates would leave their windows and back door open to let in the fresh air. The neighbourhood kids would pop into the back yard to play with Gregory in his blow-up splash pool. It was all going so well. Sue had a new boyfriend and Suzanne's sister, Amanda, had set her up with her boyfriend's brother, a sheep shearer. As the New Year beckoned, their lives were full of endless possibilities.

Easey Street is a long, straight road with small, single-storey homes fronted by white picket fences. Nothing fancy. Nothing out of the ordinary. Nothing to write home about. That was until January 1977, when all those hopes and dreams of the friends living at number 147 came to a violent end. Suzanne, by then aged 28, and Sue, 27, were savagely attacked and stabbed to death. Melbourne reeled at the horrific nature of the murders; the neighbourhood was traditionally quiet and working-class, and a place where people felt safe. The housemates were close to their friends in the city, and no doubt stay-at-home mum Suzanne saw it as the perfect place to raise her son. The last time the women were seen alive was on the evening of January 10, 1977, when Sue's brother and his girlfriend paid them a visit. Martin Bartlett had been doing his sister a favour, hooking up speakers at the three-bedroomed home. When he left at about 9pm, Gregory was asleep, and the women had settled in front of the TV to watch The Sullivans.

Sometime later that day, the killer struck. Suzanne was sexually assaulted and stabbed 25 times. Her body was left on the floor. Sue had apparently come to her friend's aid and was stabbed 55 times. The killer left her for dead in the hallway, face down. Gregory, unharmed, had been in his cot for three nights and two days, with no food or water, and his dead mother only feet away. Neighbour Ilona Stevens first heard his cries on January 11 but didn't think anything of it. Children often cry. Returning home from work that same evening, she saw Mishka, the puppy, running loose along Easey Street. She and flatmate Janet Powell caught Mishka and put her in their garden, where it could not escape again. She then popped round to Suzanne and Sue's cottage and knocked. Getting no reply, she pinned a note to the front door explaining about Mishka, and returned home. As night fell, she saw a light shining from the kitchen at the rear of the property. Seeing that the door was open, she shouted across from her garden. Again, there was no response.

The next morning, Ilona and Janet again heard the toddler crying. They knocked on the front door and got no reply. According to Helen Thomas's book, Murder on Easey Street, Ilona climbed over the back fence and entered the property, coming across Sue's body face down in the hallway by the front door. She then found Suzanne's body in the front bedroom. Gregory was still in his cot, in the small sewing room that doubled as his bedroom. Ilona's note was still pinned to the door, and there was also a note on the kitchen table from Suzanne's boyfriend, Barry Woodard. He'd left it, not realising the two women were dead merely feet away. It read: 'Ring Barry as soon as you get home'—a call that was never made. Woodard told investigators that he'd tried calling Suzanne on numerous occasions but got no reply. He then drove to the property with his brother, Henry, and left the note. The lights were on and the kitchen door was open, but even so, he ventured no further into the house. The following day, he rang again, and the call was answered. What he hadn't expected was for the police to be on the end of the line.

An intense police investigation ensued. When officers arrived at the scene, they found no signs of forced entry. What they did find, however, was a bathroom messy with bloodstains, as though the killer had tried to clean themselves or wash evidence away. The culprit had then walked out of the back door and into the night. Suspects were rounded up and questioned, including Woodard and Sue's boyfriend. It transpired that both men had entered the property at different times after the murders, and both claimed they hadn't seen the bodies or heard Gregory's cries. Twenty years later, DNA testing cleared them both.

Melbourne was stunned. The papers called it one of the most brutal sex crimes in Victoria's history. Women who lived alone were advised to keep their doors locked.

Although the case was high profile, there were other murders to investigate and only 16 detectives were assigned to Victoria's homicide squad at the time. Perhaps the police thought it would be easy to solve; there was DNA available from the crime scene, and it had happened in a home, so the victims may have known their killer. But there were no leads. Nine days after the bodies were discovered, a knife thought to have been used in the killings was found on a ramp leading to Victoria Park Railway Station. On January

14, examinations of a manhole and drains in the area recovered a bloodstained face cloth and shawl two blocks from Easey Street. Still, no arrests were made.

The inquests into the women's deaths were held before city coroner Mr. H.W. Pascoe, S.M., on July 12, 1977. The official verdict was of 'multiple stab wounds then and there feloniously unlawfully and maliciously inflicted by a person or persons unknown and that such person did murder the said deceased'. Police surmised that the murderer had entered the premises through Sue's bedroom; the blind had been dislodged and dirt was found on the end of the bed. Bloodstains were found in the bathroom and a bloodstained towel was on the couch in the lounge. There were smears of blood along the passage wall to where Sue's body lay. Suzanne's body was on the floor of her bedroom with a pool of blood under her and another about 60cm above her head. She was naked from the waist down. Her underwear and shorts were found beside the bed.

Young Gregory Armstrong went to live with his aunt, Gayle, and her family. A year after the murders, a reward of $50,000 was offered but there were still no answers forthcoming for the broken families. 'We'll never really get over this until this fellow is caught,' Gayle told reporters. "You walk around not knowing who did the murder. It could be the bloke next door.' The house in Easey Street sat empty until 1983. It went on the market again in 2011, but the passing of time did little to blunt the property's grim reputation. The Age reported that similar homes in the area sold for $600,000 or more, but number 147 was on market for $460,000 to $500,000. The sale attracted more than 100 people, many of them voyeurs who proved to be more interested in visiting the crime scene than bidding. It was never going to be an easy sell. The estate agents, Nelson Alexander, came under fire from locals and Support After Murder, a victim support group, who objected to the 'absolutely disgusting' advert for the sale. The estate agents, they said, were disrespectful to Suzanne and Sue because the advert referred to the property's place in Melbourne 'folklore'. Nelson Alexander denied attempting to profit from the house's notoriety but changed the advert's wording to 'having played its part in Melbourne history.' Under consumer laws, agents must disclose that a murder or violent crime has occurred in a property when asked a direct question, but do not have to volunteer the information. Agent Bill Batcheler said: 'We were trying to fulfill disclosure obligations. We were trying to do it as discreetly as we could and be very, very sensitive to the history of the house.' According to Peter Demiris, the owner at the time of the murders, the house was empty for almost six years before his family sold it to the then current owner in 1983. The eventual winning bidder was a young woman, and the hammer price was $571,000. In June 2017, the property was on the market again, this time for $1,095,000. It was marketed by Nelson Alexander as 'enjoying a revitalized identity with a contemporary makeover while retaining its period lustre. This classic brick Victorian boasting a fresh neutral colour palette presents an excellent opportunity to secure a slice of the increasingly popular and tightly held inner city. With high ceilings and gleaming polished concrete floors, this refurbished home comprises two generously proportioned bedrooms with pure wool carpets, living room with adjacent dining serviced by a well-appointed kitchen, refreshed bathroom and large courtyard/garden with excellent scope to extend or add. Exceptionally positioned in Collingwood's eclectic lifestyle precinct, the home is conveniently located to Victoria Park train station, buses, trams and the delights of Smith St.'

In the late 1990s, police hoped DNA testing would finally reveal the identity of the killer but eight key suspects—all of whom voluntarily provided blood samples—were cleared. A ninth suspect was later tested and also cleared. The case had become one of the homicide squad's most perplexing. In 2011, it was reopened as a cold case. There was still nothing to link the DNA, and on April 8, 2012, new tests were ordered on the original suspects—more than a decade after they'd been cleared by the exact same technology—in the hope that scientific advances in DNA profiling would help. Detective Inspector Michael Hughes told later how they had 130 'persons of interest', many from the original investigation, who they were ruling out one by one, beginning with those who were still alive. 'Of those 130 people, we know 41 people are deceased and we've made substantial inroads to the remainder of the people on those lists,' he said, adding it was unlikely that the killer had led a crime-free life for the past 40 years. 'I don't believe you can commit a crime with this brutality and go unnoticed by police, whether it be in Victoria or somewhere else,' he said, 'I think technology will catch up with him, and our persistence if he's on that list will catch up with him.'

On January 15, 2017, Victoria Police announced a $1-million bounty for information leading to a conviction, to be paid at the discretion of the Chief Commissioner of Police. Acting Sergeant Melissa Seach told the media: 'While DNA testing has not uncovered an offender thus far, it has provided a useful tool in eliminating suspects and remains a very strong line of enquiry.' Detective Inspector Hughes added: 'We are also hoping that the $1-million announcement will encourage someone out there with crucial information or direct knowledge of these murders to come forward. We believe after 40 years, someone out there knows something and it is time for them to come forward. These unsolved murders have been extremely devastating on these two young women's families and after all this time we would like to provide them with closure.'

On January 17, 2017, Tess Lawrence, contributing editor-at-large for the Independentaustralia.net website, told how, at the police's request, in January 1977 she had entered the house in Easey Street in the hope that an article might prompt the memory and conscience of someone—anyone—to then come forward with information. Police told Lawrence that the savagery and brutality of the knifings was such that the murderer would have required extraordinary strength, or blind rage, perhaps drug fuelled. 'I remember I could smell the fear,' she wrote. 'I could almost taste it. I could hear my own inner screams and sensed theirs echoing in that desolate silence where lurk the ghosts of bleak tragedy and unnatural death at the hands of our own species.' According to Lawrence, both sides of the narrow hallway was splattered with what seemed like litres of blood. She also noted that the wallpaper looked like it had been stencilled in blood by the palms, hands and fingers of someone desperately trying to defend themselves.

Since the time of the Easey Street murders there have been a number of high-profile cases in Melbourne, including the Hoddle Street Massacre, Queen Street Massacre, Walsh Street shootings of two policemen, and the murders of society and gangland figures. Hours after the murder squad arrived at Easey Street, their attention was drawn to crime reporter John Grant, who had stayed overnight at the home of Ilona Stevens, next door to the crime scene. Grant was well known to the authorities as he'd covered the crime beat for years, and detectives focused on where he had been at the time the murders took place—sleeping on a couch next door. Grant, Stevens and a third party, Janet Powell, insisted they had heard nothing unusual that night. Investigators, however, could not ignore the coincidence that the reporter was in the wrong place for the second time in two years. He had also been with American tourist Julie Ann Garciacelay when she disappeared in 1975.

Garciacelay worked as a library reference clerk. On July 1, a week before her 20th birthday, Grant and his two friends were at her apartment in Canning Street, North Melbourne, which she shared with her sister, Gail. They claim she stepped outside to make a phone call at a public box and never returned. When Gail dropped by the next day, she found a blood-soaked towel and underwear strewn around Ms Garciacelay's home. The ensuing case revolved around the presence of Grant and his friends–former boxer Rhys Collins and criminal John Joseph Power, whom Grant knew through his reporting beat. On April 11, 2018, Garciacelay was officially deemed a murder victim by Victoria's state coroner, Sara Hinchey. As police blew away the cobwebs of her missing person file, the announcement barely made it into the papers. Grant has never offered a full account in the public record of what happened on the night of her disappearance, other than that he and his friends went her apartment for a drink, and that was all. Grant was cleared of any involvement after a DNA analysis in 2010. The other two men have since died, and the case remains unsolved. Grant was also cleared of any involvement in the Easey Street murders through DNA testing.

These days, Collingwood's Easey Street is known as an enclave of art studios and galleries, as well as the home of PBS 106.7FM, a progressive radio station. Having been such music lovers, Suzanne Armstrong and Sue Bartlett would have enjoyed knowing that. What cannot be removed from this pleasant Melbourne suburb is the memory of their murders, and certainly not while the case remains open.

RESEARCH AND SOURCES

CHAPTER 1: DAVID BERKOWITZ

Thoughtco.com
Allthatsinteresting.com
Crimemuseum.org
Biography.com/crime-figure/david-berkowitz
Vice.com
Nypost.com
Cbsnews.com
Wikipedia.org
Web.archive.org
Inspiringquotes.us
Crimeandinvestigation.co.uk
Ranker.com
Newsweek.com
Associated Press
Crimemuseum.org

CHAPTER 2: THEODORE ROBERT COWELL (TED BUNDY)

Initial Brief of Appellant, in the Supreme Court of Florida, March 30, 1982 –fall.fsulawc.com/flsupct/57772/57772ini.pdf

Clarkprosecutor.org/html/death/US/bundy106.htm
Law.justia.com/cases/florida/supreme-court/1985/59128-0.html
Theodore Robert BUNDY, Petitioner-Appellant, v. Richard L.
    DUGGER, Secretary, Department of Corrections, State of Florida,
    Respondent-Appellee. No. 86-3773.
United States Court of Appeals Eleventh Circuit. July 7, 1988
Sara Kettler—Biography.com
Crimeandinvestigation.co.uk/crime-files/ted-bundy/trial
Allthatsinteresting.com
The Stranger Beside Me: The True Crime Story of Ted Bundy by
    Ann Rule
LA Times
Wikipedia.com
Esquire.com

CHAPTER 3: JOHN WAYNE GACY

Findagrave.com/memorial/3505/john-wayne-gacy—bio by Kit and
    Morgan Benson
Historicmysteries.com/john-wayne-gacy—Jim Harper, January
    26, 2016
Biography.com
Imdb.com/name/nm0300475/bio
Wikipedia.com
Criminalminds.fandom.com/wiki/John_Wayne_Gacy
Britannica.com—John Philip Jenkins
Nbcchicago.com—Phil Rogers
Sites.google.com/a/umail.iu.edu/gacyweblio/marriage-and-children
Nbcchicago.com—Phil Rogers

CHAPTER 4: ROBERT EDWARD CRANE

Fandom.com
Thefamouspeople.com
Wikipedia.com
Thecrazytourist.com

Imdb.com

Vote4bobcrane.org/biography

Vote4bobcrane.blogspot.com/2011/10/stamford-connecticut-cir-
ca-1946-bob.html

Norwalksymphony.org/about-the-orchestra

Famousbio.net/bob-crane-2589.html

Imdb.com/name/nm0012245/bio

Tv.avclub.com/hogan-s-heroes-unceremonious-finale-comes-from-th
e-era-1798237542

Phoenixnewtimes.com/arts/the-mark-of-crane-6422971–M.V. Moor-
head—July 10, 1997

Paul Rubin, April 28, 1993—Phoenixnewtimes.com/news/
the-bob-crane-murder-case-part-two-6425966

CHAPTER 5: KENNETH BIANCHI
AND ANGELO BUONO JR.

Allthatsinteresting.com

Wikipedia.com

Listverse.com

Biography.com

Findagrave.com

Dangerousminds.nelapdonline.org

Justcriminals.info

Crimeandinvestigation.co.uk

Criminalmindsfandom.com

Healthline.com

Rip-losangles.blogspot.com

Carpenoctem.tv/killers/hillside

Angelfire.com

Crimelibrary.com

Crimeweb.homestead.com

Hillside-strangler.com

Apnews.com

Cbsnews.com

latimes.com/archives/la-xpm-1985-09-18-mn-6096-story.html

CHAPTER 6: JAMES WARREN JONES

Jonestown.sdsu.edu/?page_id=33222

Learnreligions.com—what cult suicides are and why they matter—Catherine Beyer

Historytoday.com—Richard Dacendish—The Jonestown Mass Suicide

Death in the time of cult suicide—Karishma H Nandkeolyar, Gulf-news.com

Indianapublicmedia.org

Culteducation.com

Wikipedia.com

Idsnews.com

Historicindianapolis.com/the-devil-in-the-old-northside

Biography.com/crime-figure/jim-jones

Jonestown.sdsu.edu

Maebrussell.com/Jonestown/Jim%20Jones%20in%20Brazil.html

San Jose Mercury News–November 27, 1978, p. 17A

Jonestown.sdsu.edu/?page_id=31441

Bbc.co.uk/news/world-latin-america-15799345

History.com/news/jonestown-jim-jones-mass-murder-suicide–lesley kennedy

Washingtonpost.com/archive/politics/1978/11/22/indi-anapolis-to-guyana-a-jim-jones-chronology/f63dfcba-b366-4604-a672-a65320a07a1b/

Alejandra, Patar. 'Dan Mitrione, Un Maestro De La Tortura'. February 9, 2001 Clarin.com/diario/2001/09/02/i-03101.htm

Jim Hougan—'Jim Jones and the Peoples Temple'. Jimhougan.com/JimJones.html

'Jones Lived Well, Kept to Himself During Mysterious Brazil Stay'. San Jose Mercury News, November 27, 1978: 17A.

John Judge—'The Black Hole of Guyana: the Untold Story of the Jonestown Massacre'. Rat Haus Reality Press. 1985. Ratical.org/ratville/JFK/JohnJudge/Jonestown.html (also here)

Langguth, A.J. 'Torture's Teachers'. The New York Times, June 11, 1979

Reiterman, Tim, and John Jacobs. Raven—'The Untold Story of the Reverend Jim Jones and His People'. New York: Penguin Group Australia, 1987

CHAPTER 7: RODRIGO JACQUES ALCALA BUQUOR

Laweekly.com
Thought.co—Charles Montaldo
New Haven Register
Vice.com
Muderpedia.org
Wikipedia.com
History.com
Groovyhistory.com
News.com.au

CHAPTER 8: DONALD NEILSON

Crimeandinvestigation.co.uk
Wikipedia.com
Dailymail.co.uk/news/article-2078229/Why-Donald-Neilson-k-Black-Panther-died-week-aged-75-chilling-killers-criminal-history.html
The making of a psychopath: Why Donald Neilson, who died this week aged 75, was one of the most chilling killers in criminal history—By Steve Bird for the Daily Mail December 24, 2011
Birminghammail.co.uk/news/local-news/from-the-archives-heiress-in-kidnap-horror-122494
news.sky.com/story/black-panther-found-prowling-on-rooftops-in-france-11814664
Crimeandinvestigation.co.uk/article/the-night-stalker-and-black-panther—Richard Bevan
Shropshirestar.com/news/nostalgia/2016/07/21/the-black-panther-the-grim-murder-that-shook-shropshire-and-the-nation/—July 21, 2016

Yorkpress.co.uk/news/9434800.the-wrecker-of-lives/
Murderpedia.org
Stokesentinel.co.uk/news/history/
    how-black-panther-was-caught-278938
Chad.co.uk/news/
    remember-the-night-they-caught-the-black-panther-1-8038196
Lawgazette.co.uk/reviews/book-review-the-black-panther-the-trials-
    and-abductions-of-donald-neilson-/5059609.article
Bbc.co.uk/news/uk-england-19191268
Business-live.co.uk/news/local-news/
    former-reporter-harry-hawkes-remembers-3916119

CHAPTER 9: PETER SUTCLIFFE

Yorkshire.com/places/west-yorkshire/bradford/bingley
Wikipedia.com
Revolvy.com/page/Sonia-Sutcliffe
Takemeback.to/23-April-1977#.XYDBvfzTU4M
Crimehub.co.uk/index.php/Jean_Jordan_-_Yorkshire_Ripper_Victim
allthatsinteresting.com/sonia-sutcliffe-peter-sutcliffe-wife
Thefamouspeople.com/profiles/peter-sutcliffe-34350.php
Truckdrivingjobs.com/faq/
    peter-sutcliffe-a-survey-of-the-yorkshire-ripper
Truecrimeengland.wordpress.com/2019/01/21/the-yorkshire-ripper/
Thetelegraphandargus.co.uk/news/8065807.250-jobs-go-in-closure/
Execulink.com/~kbrannen/victim05.htm
Telegraph.co.uk/news/uknews/crime/7893959/Bradford-prosti-
    tute-murders-profile-of-Yorkshire-Ripper-Peter-Sutcliffe.html
Burn, Cross, Jones. Source material (quotes): "Statement Of Peter
    William Sutcliffe"
Bilton, Burn, Cross, Jones, Lavelle, Yallop. Source material (quotes):
    "Statement Of Peter William Sutcliffe"
Theguardian.com/tv-and-radio/2019/mar/27/the-yorkshire-ripper-
    files-a-very-british-crime-story-review-a-stunningly-misman-
    aged-manhunt

CHAPTER 10: PEDRO ALONSO LÓPEZ

9news.com.au/world/pedro-lopez
Reddit.com—Documentaries Pedro Alonso Lopez: (Monster of the
  Andes) Serial Killer Documentary SKD
Criminalminds.fandom.com
Pearson, Nick. 'World's Second Worst Serial Killer Walked Free from
  Prison'. 9News Breaking News, 9News, December 5, 2018
Serena, Katie. 'Serial Killer Who Murdered 300 People Was Released
  From Jail, And No One Knows Where He Is.'. Allthatsinteresting.
  com—November 30, 2018
'The Monster Of The Andes: South American Serial Killer Pedro
  Lopez'. Did You Know? July 17, 2017
Wikipedia.com
Charles Montaldo—Thoughtco.com
Dr Dirk Gibson—Serial Killers Around the World: The Global
  Dimensions of Serial Murder
Health Psychology Consultancy blog post on López
Biography.com/crime-figure/pedro-alonso-lopez
Historydaily.org
People.howstuffworks.com/serial-killer6.htm

CHAPTER 11: HARVEY AND
JEANNETTE CREWE

Police.govt.nz/sites/default/files/publications/crewe-review-final-re-
  port.pdf
Stuff.co.nz
Reddit.com
Wikipedia.org
Newzealandnow.govt.nz
Waikatoregion.govt.nz
Nzherald.co.nz
Wantedknown.tumblr.com/post/41777705187/murder-at-pukekawa
Janmeecham.wordpress.com
Briefingroom.typepad.com/crewes

New Zealand Police Crewe Homicide Investigation Review, 2014 by
    Detective Superintendent Andrew J Lovelock
Report of the Royal Commission to Inquire into the Circumstances
    of the Convictions of Arthur Allan Thomas for the Murders of
    David Harvey Crewe and Jeannette Lenore Crewe, 1980
Forensic History: Crimes, Frauds, and Scandals" by Professor Eliza-
    beth A Murray

CHAPTER 12: SUZANNE ARMSTRONG
AND SUSAN BARTLETT

Heraldsun.com
Makingfutures.net
Wikipedia.com
ABC News
Trove.nia.gov.ua
Thatslife.com.au
Wikipedia.com
Finder.com.au
Pressreader.com
Findagrave.com
Abc.net.au
Twistedhistory.net.au
Reddit.com
Bullhorn.fm